Olly
drin
writ
Mar
up s
boo
his popular podcast *A Glass With...*,
interviewing international guests
ranging from P!NK to Kylie Minogue,
and appears regularly as wine
expert on BBC1's *Saturday Kitchen*.
Olly is the author of six books
including *Home Cocktail Bible* (2021).

For Ellie, a traveller in kind

World Cocktail Atlas

Travel the WORLD of DRINKS
without LEAVING your HOME

OLLY SMITH

photography by Matt Russell
cover typography by Kate Forrester

Hardie Grant

QUADRILLE

Managing Director: Sarah Lavelle

Recipe Developer: Seb Munsch

Copy Editor: Euan Ferguson

Designer: Alicia House

Photographer: Matt Russell

Drink Stylist: Loïc Parisot

Prop Stylist: Max Robinson

Cover typography: Kate Forrester

Head of Production: Stephen Lang

Senior Production Controller: Martina Georgieva

First published in 2023 by Quadrille,
an imprint of Hardie Grant Publishing

Quadrille
52–54 Southwark Street
London SE1 1UN
quadrille.com

Cataloguing in Publication Data: a catalogue record
for this book is available from the British Library.

978 1 78713 956 5

Printed in China

CONTENTS

INTRODUCTION

Although this book is about liquid, the cocktail recipes on these pages are determined by land and continent. Defined by the oceans that surround them, memories of rivers flowing through them, glaciers carving them up and peaks rising and tumbling from above, these are the sources giving rise to the world's favourite cocktails. Every drink in this book springs in part thanks to a prized ingredient born of a unique sense of place, as well as the creativity of the people who've shaken and mixed these cocktails ready for you to recreate my versions with a style of your own.

In the same way that each cocktail brings its own distinct tale of origin, they invite us to blend, cross over and create opportunities for new flavours and ways to mark a moment. Cocktails have always looked joyful to me but there's also a certain delight in the feeling they bring, whether it's unwinding into a slow, reflective drink or knocking up a neon gem for a party. The most thrilling moment is without question serving them to someone else, which is how the chain of experimentation and enjoyment continues. Feel free to tweak these recipes to suit your own specifications – the cocktail always comes from somewhere, but always leads to you.

To those corners of the world that may be missed in this collection, I cannot wait to discover ever more flavours and combinations. The real joy of making and recreating cocktails from around the world is, after all, the next recipe.

Here's to you.

AFRICA
The birthplace of humankind and the second largest continent on Earth, with almost certainly more languages spoken than any other and a quarter forested, Africa is a living treasury of epic scale. Agriculture plays a huge role, giving rise to a complex choice of ingredients that in turn leads to some of the most exciting discoveries in this book. With liqueurs and spirits of stellar allure, from the islands to the mainland, Africa is unfurling some of the most dynamic recipes of all, with seemingly endless nuances of scrumptiousness to encounter.

ANTARCTICA
Kingdom of the Freezer, locked around the South Pole, the land itself is beneath a frozen sheet some 2,000 metres (6,561 feet) thick, which accounts for around 90 per cent of the world's glacial ice. With a land area of 5.5 million square miles (14 million square feet), technically it's divided into East and West Antarctica, and offshore is teeming with life from fish to penguins and congregations of soaring seabirds. Holding the record for the lowest temperature ever registered – an impressive minus 89.2°C on 21 July 1983 – it seems only fitting that this section of the book is entirely dedicated to improving your cocktails with the essential ingredient to so many cocktail recipes... ice.

ASIA
More than five times larger than Australia, Asia is the largest continent of all. I don't have a favourite continent, but if I did – in secret – I might whisper Asia's name fondly. With the Pacific, Indian and Arctic Oceans at its limits,

the Earth's lowest point, the Dead Sea (around 430 metres/1,410 feet below sea level), and its highest, Chomolungma (Mount Everest), reaching above 8,848 metres (29,028 feet) and still rising, this is a continent of dreamy extremes. With ingredients, Asia embraces limitless invigoration for cocktail creativity. I've lived in Indonesia, and I adore the extraordinarily powerful recipes and precise flavours all across Asia that inspire curiosity with a spirit of flair and innovation. For cocktails, Asia is endlessly inventive and always encouraging.

EUROPE

Fjords, islands, oceans, lakes and seaside... I always think of Europe, the world's second smallest continent, as a place of intimate corners. Its filigree cultural kaleidoscope and industrial heritage is a fascinating lens through which cocktails past and present into focus. Glaciers, rivers and lakes have always been generous with supplying pure water for people to build and create a whole lexicon of extraordinary drinks, from liqueurs and spirits to beer and wine. The settings and mood surrounding these drinks is a giant historical fancy-dress party from glassware to pubs, clubs and bars. Calibrating your drinking with the perfect setting to match your mood is a hoot.

OCEANIA

Australia itself is the sixth largest country in the world and technically the smallest continent. From the Indian Ocean to the Pacific and into Oceania, the islands and reefs and the beauty of New Zealand's natural landscape all contribute to this wide water world with endless pockets of sunny splendour. Of course, tropical cocktails with a certain beachside vibe feature here, plus mixes from bars steeped in the informal magic of hanging out Down Under also give that instant 'time off' feeling that money can't buy. Around here, everyone is welcome and the drinks are all cool!

NORTH AMERICA

North America has breathtaking mountains and rivers and is bordered by bodies of water almost all the way around – it makes my heart sing from the Bering Sea off Alaska to the Panama Canal in the south. With the Caribbean islands as well as Greenland – the world's largest island – North America is a geographical collection of greatest hits for any cocktail fan. And when you throw in the music, dance and gigs that have grown up around cocktail culture, it's as though we have landed in a sky far beyond the Land of Oz where the law is built on just one word: 'pleasure'.

SOUTH AMERICA

Wild, cool and fizzing with the maritime mayhem of Cape Horn in the south, the continent of South America gradually warms into tropical vibrancy as you head north. The Caribbean Sea, plus the Atlantic and Pacific Oceans, define the shape of this fourth largest continent with the world's largest drainage basin, the Amazon, flowing alongside seismic rumbling and an abiding sense that anything could happen if you sip from the right glass. Mount Aconcagua, reaching higher than 6,960 metres (22,834 feet), is the tallest peak in the Southern Hemisphere, and deep within the landscape, extraordinary mineral resources are kept in tension. When unleashed in its full spectrum of brilliance, this continent is a place of cocktails dancing with delight. Let spontaneity and splendour be your guide.

CAPSULE COCKTAIL CABINET

Vodka

Rum

Tequila

Gin

Brandy

Simple syrup

Sparkling wine

White wine

Red wine

Dry vermouth

Sweet vermouth

Campari

Triple sec or Cointreau

Apricot brandy

Peach schnapps

Blue curaçao

Orange curaçao

Crème de cassis

Grenadine

St-Germain elderflower liqueur

Amaretto almond liqueur

Kahlúa coffee liqueur

Baileys Irish Cream

Crème de menthe

Angostura bitters

KIT

Shaker
A shaker is the single most useful piece of equipment for cocktail making – if you can find an insulated one, so much the better for keeping those cocktails icy-cold.

Strainer
This is a mini-sieve that will filter out bits of fruit or ice to achieve an ultra-smooth texture.

Long bar spoon
A long-handled bar spoon enables you to get to the very bottom of a shaker or tall glass to stir up the contents.

Peeler
By far the easiest way to make those impressive strips of lemon and orange zest that top the perfect cocktail is with an ordinary potato peeler. No knife or chopping board necessary!

Squeezer
This is useful but not essential – it's handy for fresh limes and lemons, but you can always use your hands and a firm squeeze!

Muddler
This is like a pestle, usually made of wood, and used to bash up spices or tenderize fruit. You could use the end of a rolling pin (with care!).

Corkscrew
Everyone has their own emergency method for getting into a bottle of beer or wine when on a picnic with no corkscrew, but let's face it, this bit of kit is jolly handy.

GLASSWARE

Wine glass
Don't rush out and buy any new wine glasses for cocktails – you'll want something with a large bowl as most cocktails served in wine glasses will probably also feature ice (such as spritzes), and perhaps fruit and herbs, so the glass needs to be roomy.

Hurricane
These can vary in shape, but a hurricane is usually a tall tumbler with a low bowl and a flared rim, used for serving mixed and fruity drinks like a Piña Colada.

Rocks/Old Fashioned
A rocks glass is a stocky, chunky tumbler, most recognizable as the classic whisky glass. A standard tumbler is medium-height and flat-based, and can be either straight-sided, flared or curved.

Shot
A shot glass or shooter traditionally contains a single measure of spirit, but since single or measured quantities vary according to where in the world you live, there is no standard size of glass. To make the shot-based cocktails in this book you'll want enough volume to contain a couple of measures.

Collins
This is usually a straight-sided, tall tumbler with enough volume and height to contain lots of ice, also referred to as a highball glass.

Coupe
The traditional coupe shape is the classic stemmed 'belle époque' Champagne glass, since replaced in popularity by the taller flute. 'Coupe' means 'cup', and it's that curved, elegant shape that's so visually appealing when you serve a cocktail.

Martini
The martini glass is the quintessential cocktail glass – stemmed, with a triangular, straight-edged bowl, it's perfect for so many types of drinks and you'll definitely be needing one or two. Or three, or four...

Flute
Elegant flute glasses come in many subtly different shapes – they need to be tall and thin to prevent all those beautiful bubbles escaping.

Speciality
Occasionally a drink calls for a glass with a handle, usually because it's a hot punch or a frosty beverage like a Mint Julep. And sometimes you'll want a tall pitcher of a batch cocktail, to refrigerate and pour at your leisure.

GARNISHES

Fruit
A twist, peel or slice of a fruit like lemon, orange or lime can make all the difference – that final spritz of citrus oil that brings the cocktail together. If you like, you can flash with a blowtorch or lighter – or just give your peel a little squeeze as you drop it into the drink.

To make a citrus flag garnish, take half a slice of fruit, push a cocktail stick through the pith on one side, spear a cocktail cherry and push the stick back through the pith on the other side.

Maraschino cherries
Ah, the glorious maraschino cherry, a vital component of cocktails like the Manhattan; maraschino liqueur itself is an essential in so many drinks. Pop them onto a cocktail stick, or in the bottom of a martini glass for a sweet treat when you get to the bottom. Slurp!

Olives
Essential for the savoury rush of the famous Dirty Martini, small green olives are for the cocktail connoisseur – they need to be stone-in for authenticity and maximum flavour.

Cocktail onions and pickles
We're into serious savoury territory here – a Gibson would just be a Martini without an onion, and a pickle on the side of your Bloody Mary will make it a super-sensation of sweet, sour, salty and savoury.

Salt
Not just for a Margarita, creating an impressive salt rim is easy as pie – cover a small plate with salt, take a wedge of fruit (usually lime) and rub it around the edge of your glass. Place it upturned in the salt and, hey presto.

Herb sprigs and dried flowers
Herbs and flowers make a wonderfully aromatic and attractive garnish – you'll be familiar with mint in a Mojito but basil, thyme and rosemary are also magical ingredients. Use the softest leaves from the tip of the stalk. Dried rose petals look striking scattered over a drink, too.

 Fruit

 Herbal

 Floral

 Savoury

 Nuts and spices

 Miscellany

SYRUPS

SIMPLE SYRUP

500ml (17oz) water

500g (17oz) golden caster sugar

Mix the water and sugar together in a pan

Once the sugar has dissolved, cover and simmer for 15 minutes

Decant into a sealable, sterilized bottle or container

Allow to cool completely before use

Will store for up to a month

You can use either golden caster sugar or regular white caster sugar.

Simple syrup is the most commonly used syrup in cocktails and is a 1:1 ratio. This simple syrup recipe forms the base of many other syrups.

If you like a sweeter, more concentrated syrup, you can make a 2:1 ratio (sugar to water) syrup.

It's really easy to make, and like all the syrups listed here, you can make smaller or larger amounts depending on what you need – just adjust the quantities in proportion.

For **herb syrups**, add a small handful of herbs to the mixture as you're heating it, so the flavours can infuse. Strain through a sieve before decanting.

For **cinnamon syrup**, add a cinnamon stick to the mixture while heating. Leave to cool and infuse before straining and decanting.

For **vanilla syrup**, add a vanilla pod to the mixture. Leave to cool and infuse before straining and decanting.

For **rose syrup**, add 1 tbsp rose water to the mixture.

GRENADINE

500ml (17oz) pomegranate juice

500g (17oz) golden caster sugar

2 dashes orange blossom water

Heat the pomegranate juice and sugar in a pan

Once the sugar has dissolved, cover loosely and simmer gently for 15 minutes

Add the orange blossom water and decant into a sealable, sterilized bottle or container

Allow to cool completely before use

Will store for up to a month

SPICED GINGER

500ml (17oz) water

500g (17oz) golden caster sugar

20g (¾oz) root ginger, roughly sliced

2 tsp coriander seeds

1 tsp cumin seeds

4 cardamom pods, lightly crushed

½ tsp ground turmeric

Heat the water and the sugar together in a pan until the sugar dissolves

Add the spices, cover and simmer gently for 15 minutes

Take off the heat and leave to cool

Leave the mixture to infuse for 24 hours

Pass through a fine sieve or muslin cloth and decant into a sealable, sterilized bottle or container

Will store for up to a month

DEMERARA

500ml (17oz) water

500g (17oz) demerara sugar

Heat the water and the sugar together in a pan

Once the demerara sugar has dissolved, cover and simmer gently for 15 minutes

Decant into a sealable, sterilized bottle or container

Allow to cool completely before use

Will store for up to a month

Very similar to simple syrup, but the demerara sugar adds a mellow, toasted flavour to drinks.

HONEY

540ml (18oz) water

540ml (18oz) runny honey

Heat the water and the honey together gently – it's important you do not let it boil

Once the honey and water are well combined, cover and simmer for 5 minutes

Decant into a sealable, sterilized bottle or container

Allow to cool completely before use

Will store for up to a month

As an added bonus, if you have a cold or sore throat, this works really nicely heated up with a little extra hot water and the juice of half a lemon. A dash of whisky also helps! Add some cloves and a cinnamon stick to make a traditional hot toddy.

TONKA BEAN

500ml (17oz) water

500g (17oz) golden caster sugar

6-8 tonka beans

Heat the water and the sugar together in a pan

Once the sugar has dissolved, cover and simmer for 15 minutes

Lightly crush the tonka beans and add to the syrup

Leave to infuse for 24 hours

Pass through a fine sieve or muslin cloth and decant into a sealable, sterilized bottle or container

Will store for up to a month

You can add more or fewer tonka beans to taste. While they're not yet readily available in supermarkets, there are lots of online food specialists that stock them. If you can't get a hold of any, vanilla makes a good substitute – you don't get quite the same nuttiness coming through but it's still delicious.

BARA BRITH

500ml (17oz) water

500g (17oz) golden caster sugar

2 cinnamon sticks

2 cloves

½ tsp allspice

¼ tsp ground ginger

¼ tsp ground mace

¼ tsp ground coriander

¼ tsp ground nutmeg

Heat the water and the sugar together in a pan

Once the sugar has dissolved, add the spices, then cover and simmer gently for 15 minutes

Leave to infuse for 24 hours

Pass through a fine sieve or muslin cloth and decant into a sealable, sterilized container

Will store for up to a month

As well as using it in the Bara Brith Sour (see page 178), try adding this syrup to a cup of tea.

ROSEMARY

500ml (17oz) water

500g (17oz) golden caster sugar

2 sprigs rosemary

Heat the water and the sugar together in a pan

Once the sugar has dissolved, add the rosemary, then cover and simmer gently for 15 minutes

Leave to infuse for 24 hours

Pass through a fine sieve or muslin and decant into a sealable, sterilized bottle or container

Will store for up to a month

This recipe can be used for any woody herbs, including thyme.

ANTARCTICA

REALM OF ICE

It's the only continent that's virtually uninhabited, covering around 20 per cent of the Southern Hemisphere, larger than both Europe and Oceania, with no countries – though several nations lay claim to it. Welcome to Antarctica, realm of ice.

The Antarctic ice sheet is the largest single piece of ice on planet Earth, at the time of writing, 14 million square kilometres (5.4 million square miles). That's a whole lot of coldness for your cocktail creations. But there's so much more to ice than just cooling down your drink.

Ice is for:

- Chilling
- Adjusting texture
- Diluting
- Creating visual appeal

There are many different shapes and sizes of ice. The pros, cons and subtle variations are hotly debated, but the most common forms of ice are:

STANDARD ICE CUBES

The workhorses of the ice world, used for just about everything. Make sure they're fresh from the freezer: nobody wants sloppy, wet ice over-diluting their drink. Standard cubes work best in long drinks and are the perfect ice to add to your mixing glass when you're stirring a Martini.

LARGE CUBES

Larger cubes work well in lowball glasses – they melt more slowly than standard cubes so won't dilute your drink quite as much. They're also great for shaking cocktails, but avoid for stirring as they won't melt enough to add the required level of dilution.

OVERSIZED BALLS AND CUBES

Giant balls and cubes offer both style and substance. They're perfect for short drinks that you want to sip and take your time over without becoming watered down. And they're also great for large punch bowls of cocktails that might be sitting around or even topped up over several hours. Try adding sliced fruit to the balls or cubes for a more visually pleasing way of keeping punches and pitchers of drinks cool.

CRUSHED ICE

Crushed ice gives texture and just the right amount of dilution to certain types of cocktail. Use in Juleps, Brambles and any slushy-style drinks. Crushed ice has a larger surface area so cools more quickly and dilutes spirits to ensure high levels of refreshment. It also makes blending frozen drinks a whole lot easier.

ICE STICKS

Long ice spears or tall, thin, rectangular blocks are a great addition for keeping long drinks cold without diluting them. They also look great when you add edible flowers, berries or herbs.

FUN WITH ICE

Ice doesn't just have to go in your drinks. You can design your own ice-based creations: ice shot glasses, ice luges, ice buckets made of ice, ice mugs or large ice punch bowls with festive frozen garlands to float on top.

You can even buy silicone moulds for just about anything, but it's worth experimenting with making your own.

The simplest method is to find two plastic containers – one to create the outer shell and a slightly smaller one for the inner.

- Fill the outer container half full of water, then add any extras like fruit, edible flowers, herbs, flowers, herbs, berries, gold leaf... the possibilities are endless.

- Put the first container in the freezer then float the middle container on top and weigh it down so that it sits low in the water (duct tape often comes in handy to keep it in place).

- Once fully frozen, remove from the freezer and run the containers under warm water to remove your icy creation.

To make wreaths, just fill the lower part of a bundt tin with water and decorations. It then pops out in a ring shape.

Try experimenting with different shapes and varying the amount of water to create something unique and special!

CLEAR ICE

It's debatable as to what difference it makes to the taste, but the gold standard for ice is beautifully sparkling crystal-clear ice.

It's the impurities and air bubbles in water that give ice a slightly cloudy appearance. To get these out you need to freeze the water slowly. You can buy directional-freezing ice trays that produce clear ice, or with a bit of practice you can try one of these two methods.

Boiling method:
Boil the water once, allow to cool, boil a second time and let it cool to lukewarm, then freeze in ice cube trays.

Cooler method:
Fill a small, very clean food storage container with water (ideally boil the water first and allow it to cool to lukewarm). Don't place a lid on the container, but pop it straight into the

freezer and leave to freeze for around 20-24 hours (freezing time depends on how much water you're freezing).

The ice block should be watery underneath – the top layers freeze first, pushing the impurities downwards. Discard the water and you'll be left with a nice clear block. If you freeze for too long and part of your block is cloudy, don't worry – just cut away the clear ice to use.

Cutting ice blocks can be dangerous so do take great care. Place the ice block on a clean tea towel, carefully score with a serrated knife then chip away with a pick or chisel to create large cubes or slices of ice.

A FINAL NOTE ON ICE

If there's just one thing you should remember about ice, it's this: if the ice is floating in your glass, you need to add more ice!

Africa

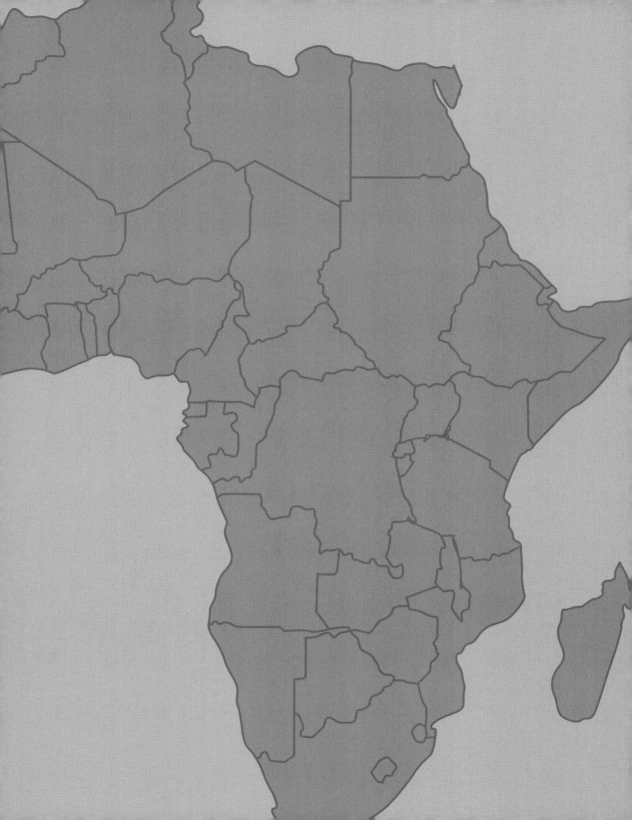

THE TEJ
COCKTAIL

ETHOPIA

A core ingredient for tej is honey, the blessing of the bees. If tracking down tej is proving elusive, try using mead: Gosnells of London is a good bet. With tej, a little bit of herby spice comes along for the ride as well as the natural sweetness and depth of honey – which of course offers a wide range of flavours and textures depending on which flowers the bees have been foraging. Mellow honey always duets beautifully with spiced rum, and in this cocktail both are lifted by lemon juice and given a brisk blast of bubbles. Liquid pizazz!

60ml (2oz) tej

60ml (2oz) spiced rum

30ml (1oz) freshly squeezed lemon juice

Soda water to top

Ice: Cubed

Garnish: Orange-cherry flag

Equipment: Cocktail shaker, strainer

Fill a cocktail shaker with ice

Add all the ingredients except the soda water

Shake vigorously to combine and chill

Strain into a collins glass filled with ice

Top with soda water

Garnish with an orange-cherry flag

COCONUT DAIQUIRI

Simple to memorize, easy to assemble and always a massive hit at parties, the Coconut Daiquiri gives that hedonistic feeling of a tropical cove with an inviting bassline dancing on the breeze. Alongside its great rum, Mauritius is a treasury of tasty ingredients – notably coconuts, which taste lush when infused into the silky local spirit. This is the ultimate cocktail for transporting your brain to the beach – as you sip, close your eyes and the emerald ocean will be rolling up those pearly sands before you take your next one.

30ml (1oz) Green Island superior light Mauritius rum

30ml (1oz) Mauritius Dodo coconut rum

30ml (1oz) freshly squeezed lime juice

30ml (1oz) cream of coconut

Ice: Cubed

Garnish: Lime twist

Equipment: Cocktail shaker, strainer

Fill a cocktail shaker with ice

Add all ingredients and shake vigorously to combine and chill

Strain into a chilled cocktail or coupe glass

Garnish with a twist of lime

MILK TART COCKTAIL

(A.K.A. SOUTH AFRICAN MILK TART)

SOUTH AFRICA

I first came across the Milk Tart Cocktail on a wine-tasting visit to South Africa: it is lighter than you might expect, and inspired by the famous local milky tart pud. Try serving it after dinner instead of dessert for a brilliant mood booster – this recipe will make about 20 shots. Also perfect for a party or even as an opening drink for a boozy brunch.

300ml (10oz) vanilla vodka

1 can (410g) evaporated milk

1 can (397g) condensed milk

Garnish: Ground cinnamon

Equipment: Blender

Add all the ingredients to a blender cup and blend to combine (you can also whisk together in a bowl)

Transfer to a sealable bottle or container and refrigerate for at least 1 hour

Serve into frozen shot glasses

Garnish with a light dusting of ground cinnamon

FRESH PEPPERMINT LEMONADE

BENIN

A jolt of peppermint to the palate is akin to a lightning strike jumpstarting the mind. One sip of this invigorating cocktail is enough to kickstart a dazzling constellation across your internal horizon. Like a flashbulb in a pristine pool, I adore the dazzling delight of Fresh Peppermint Lemonade, whether I'm surrounded by frosty peaks that echo the bracing chill or luxuriating in warm golden sunlight and cooling off within.

45ml (1½oz) sodabi

60ml (2oz) freshly squeezed lemon juice

15ml (½oz) peppermint syrup

Soda water to top

Ice: Crushed

Garnish: Peppermint sprig and lemon twist

Equipment: Long bar spoon

Three-quarters fill a glass with crushed ice

Add the sobadi, lemon juice and peppermint syrup

Stir gently to combine

Top with soda water

Cap with a scoop of crushed ice

Garnish with a peppermint sprig and a twist of lemon

For a variation on this recipe, try taking a stopover in Cuba and switch sodabi for golden rum, which gives an alternative detonation of deliciousness.

DAWA

KENYA

The healing power of honey is legendary. Depending what kind of honey you use, this drink will be influenced by its complexities, nuances and subtleties. You can buy dawa sticks online, but in general anything coated in honey will do the trick. When the honey stick hits the ice it seizes up, and slowly releases sweetness as you sip.

Variations on the Dawa are plentiful, but the core principles always involve a certain amount of sweetness, plenty of zippy refreshment and a sense of balance. That sense of proportion is why it's among my favourite cocktails to enjoy with the give and take of a leisurely conversation.

In Swahili, dawa means 'medicine', and if you enjoy a Caipirinha (see page 30), you'll have a healthy appreciation for this Dawa, my prescription for your new favourite cocktail.

60ml (2oz) vodka

2 tsp demerara sugar

¾ of a fresh lime, cut into 3 pieces

Kenyan honey (or acacia for an alternative)

Ice: Crushed

Garnish: Dawa stick (a cocktail stirring stick covered in honey)

Equipment: Muddler, long bar spoon

Add the lime pieces and sugar to a collins glass and muddle

Pour in the vodka and stir gently to combine

Fill the glass with crushed ice

Dip your dawa stick into the honey and drop into the cocktail, then stir gently

BENIN
BLUSH

BENIN

The flourish of fruit blended with spice sends my tail feathers into a frenzy. If you can't find spiced sodabi, spiced rum presents an alternative trajectory to plot for your palate. Either way, it's worth taking the time to freshly juice your fruit to maximize vitality. Whether it's for a sunrise brunch or mellow sundowner, this blushing beauty is a keeper from dawn to dusk.

45ml (1½oz) spiced sodabi

45ml (1½oz) freshly squeezed orange juice

45ml (1½oz) freshly squeezed pineapple juice

7.5ml (¼oz) freshly squeezed lime juice

Dash of grenadine (or grenadine syrup; see page 12)

Soda water to top

Ice: Cubed and crushed

Garnish: Dehydrated orange slice

Equipment: Cocktail shaker, strainer

Fill a cocktail shaker with ice cubes

Add the sodabi, orange, pineapple and lime juice

Shake vigorously to combine and chill

Strain into a hurricane glass three-quarters filled with crushed ice

Top with soda water and drop the grenadine through the cocktail

Garnish with a slice of dehydrated orange

AFRICAN LULLABY

If like me you're a lifelong fan of *The Big Lebowski*, this classic will lap fondly at the frontier of your deepest dreams. In that cult movie Jeff Bridges plays Jeff Lebowski, also known as The Dude, whose favourite drink is a White Russian and who lulls himself into a slumber by listening to a cassette of bowling sounds. Instead of instant karma, this drink is instant calmer – try it the morning after the night before instead of your regular Bloody Mary for a totally different and delicious approach to a cascade of comfort. In fact, deploy this at any time to just feel more like The Dude, and whatever you do, 'Just take it easy, man.'

45ml (1½oz) Amarula cream liqueur

15ml (½oz) coconut milk

75ml (2½oz) milk

¼ tsp grated nutmeg

Ice: Crushed

Garnish: Whipped cream and cocktail cherry

Equipment: Blender

Add all the ingredients to a blender cup with 1 scoop of crushed ice

Blend on high until you have a smooth, thick cocktail

Tap out into a wine glass

Garnish with a swirl of whipped cream and a cocktail cherry on top

NIGERIAN CHAPMAN

(NON-ALCOHOLIC)

NIGERIA

As fruity as it is fabulous, the Nigerian Chapman instantly evokes days of warmth and wonder. A treat for summer days, it's a go-to for garden sipping or refreshment in the park – and a sugar-free soda drink also works well here if it floats your boat. Of course, if you fancy lacing your Nigerian Chapman with booze, a vodka glug or rum splash can be lush, and I've also enjoyed it with a jolt of gin. But booze-free, served in a chilled glass, is the classic and absolutely excellent way for me. And instead of plain ice cubes, I love freezing the lemon-lime soda to release even more fruitiness as they melt. Invisible impact!

750ml (25oz) fizzy orange soda

750ml (25oz) lemon-lime soda

90ml (3oz) grenadine (or grenadine syrup; see page 12)

10-12 dashes Angostura bitters

4 slices cucumber

4 slices lemon

4 slices lime

Small handful of mint

Ice: Cubed

Garnish: Mint sprig

Equipment: Long bar spoon

Add 4 large slices of cucumber, lemon, lime and a small handful of mint to a pitcher

Fill to half with cubed ice

Add the remaining ingredients and stir with a long bar spoon

Top up the pitcher with more ice if needed

Pour into eight chilled glasses and garnish each with a sprig of mint

CABO VERDE CAIPIRINHA

This is a citrus sensation. Lime takes the grogue by the scruff of the neck and lifts it into skies of sublime refreshment. Similar to that feeling of fine sand and sea soothing between your toes, the laidback yet focused Cabo Verde Caipirinha is impossible to resist. And just in case you're wondering, grogue is the treasured local spirit made from sugar cane. If you can't find it, use cachaça or white rum instead. And get ready to chill!

60ml (2oz) grogue

¾ of a lime, cut into 3 pieces

2 tsp sugar

Ice: Crushed

Garnish: Lime twist

Equipment: Muddler, long bar spoon

Place the lime pieces and sugar into the bottom of a collins glass and muddle

Three-quarters fill the glass with crushed ice

Pour the grogue into the glass and churn gently with a bar spoon to combine

Cap with crushed ice

Garnish with a twist of lime

CAPE SNOW

SOUTH AFRICA

Van der Hum liqueur erupts from the Cape wine lands of South Africa with its distinctive tangerine zing and wafting fragrant spice tickling the breeze of inspiration. In this cold conundrum of a drink, it's boosted with brandy and smoothed over with vanilla ice cream, becoming as textural as it is dynamic. While any decent South African brandy will do, for this cocktail, check out Copper Republic's Honeybush Wood Finish – and for further exploration, keep an eye out for the excellent aged brandies from wineries such as Kaapzicht and Tokara. If Van der Hum is proving elusive, you can switch it out for Grand Marnier or Cointreau.

30ml (1oz) Van der Hum tangerine liqueur

30ml (1oz) brandy

2 scoops vanilla ice cream

Ice: Crushed

Garnish: Dehydrated orange slice

Equipment: Blender

Add all the ingredients to a blender cup with half a scoop of crushed ice

Blend on high until you have a smooth, thick cocktail

Tap out into a wine glass

Garnish with a dehydrated slice of orange

ROOIBOS TEA PUNCH

(NON-ALCOHOLIC)

SOUTH AFRICA

I'm a massive fan of rooibos tea. I first tasted it when I was a student at Edinburgh University and worked at the Cameo cinema in Tollcross. There was a café across the road called Ndebele (now closed) and I spent many a happy break reading my book, meeting perfect strangers and lapping up the curious conviviality of the uniquely earthy-fruity balance of the rooibos. I used to love my rooibos tea with a swirl of honey, and here in this non-alcoholic punch, the fruit very much plays the same role, sweetening, enlivening and enriching the leaves of the splendid South African bush. And if you're up for the full party-punch effect, add 90ml (3oz) of vodka and crank up the stereo.

600ml (20oz) strong brewed rooibos tea, cooled

600ml (20oz) peach juice

6 strawberries

10 raspberries

1 peach, stoned and sliced

1 lemon, sliced

Soda water to top

Ice: Cubed

Garnish: Peach slices, chopped strawberries and lemon wheels

Equipment: Long bar spoon

Fill a pitcher with ice

Add all the ingredients except the soda water

Stir to combine with a long bar spoon

Top with soda water and stir once more

Pour into frozen punch glasses

SEYCHELLOISE

SEYCHELLES

Exotic and easy as a tropical sunbeam, this cocktail is the taste of long days wearing flip-flops and a leisurely lust for taking it easy. Named after the local takamaka tree, the rum is blended with locally grown fruit and spices; when mixed with mango and papaya juice in this cocktail, it's as if a sun lounger has appeared to drift you into a golden daydream.

45ml (1½oz) Takamaka dark spiced rum

90ml (3oz) mango and papaya juice

15ml (½oz) freshly squeezed lime juice

Ice: Cubed and crushed

Garnish: Lime wedge

Equipment: Cocktail shaker

Fill a cocktail shaker with ice

Add all the ingredients and shake hard to combine and chill

Pour into a collins glass three-quarters filled with crushed ice

Cap with crushed ice

Garnish with a wedge of lime

TI PUNCH

MAURITIUS

If you enjoy a Daiquiri, are partial to an Old Fashioned or adore a Caipirinha, this is the cocktail for you. With funky sweetness, luscious texture and a zesty edge, it's a tantalizing trilogy in a single sip. Rhum agricole is made from sugar-cane juice rather than deep, dark molasses and stylistically tends to be more on the herbaceous, light and refreshing side of things. It's the sort of flavour that perfectly evokes both the feeling of being somewhere warmly exotic as well as rolling around in a grassy fresh meadow all at once. Sugar cane is, after all, a bit like massive grass and has a delightful complexity, almost a funky twist, while squeezing the lime wheel unleashes both juice and oils – releasing a roar of refreshment.

60ml (2oz) rhum agricole

7.5ml (¼oz) sugar-cane syrup

Ice: Large cubed

Garnish: Lime wedge (traditionally a chunk from the side of the lime would be used)

Add the rhum and sugar cane syrup to an old fashioned glass

Squeeze the lime between your thumb and forefinger over the glass and drop in

Add a large ice cube (or 2 regular) and stir gently to combine

SODABITINI

Sodabi's origins are immersed in war, controversy and resistance. For years a version of the drink had been created locally from fermented palm sap and infused with roots, fruits and herbs. The French colonial administration armed Beninese soldiers – including a certain Bonou Kiti Sodabi – for the fight in Europe during the First World War. Intrigued by the distilling he saw there, he began distilling palm wine from local ingredients with his brother Gbehlaton upon his return home. In 1931, the French banned local production – some suggested the quality wasn't uniform, others that the colonists wanted to promote consumption of their own liqueurs. The Sodabi brothers were imprisoned and local production continued underground in defiance of the ban. It wasn't until 1975, 15 years after Benin's independence, that the ban was finally lifted and permits were issued for sodabi production. Here's to the creativity and determination of the Sodabi brothers – and the freedom to drink whatever we choose.

45ml (1½oz) sodabi

22.5ml (¾oz) apple liqueur

22.5ml (¾oz) freshly squeezed apple juice

15ml (½oz) freshly squeezed lemon juice

15ml (½oz) honey

Ice: Cubed

Garnish: Apple slice

Equipment: Cocktail shaker, strainer

Fill a cocktail shaker with ice

Add all the ingredients

Shake vigorously to combine and chill

Strain into a chilled Y-shaped/coupe glass

Garnish with a thin slice of apple

PUMULANI COCKTAIL

MALAWI

It's hard to beat a cold frosted beer mug for instant relaxation. As soon as your fingers grasp the handle, pleasure is at hand. The blue of this cocktail is irresistible to the eye, the cool of the glass tingles the grip, and the sweet heat of aromatic ginger with the orange impact of curaçao and mellow coconut rum elide into a spiral of scrumptiousness. The name Pumulani translates as 'rest well' from the Chichewa language in Malawi, and sinking into one of these promotes exactly that.

30ml (1oz) coconut rum

15ml (½oz) blue curaçao

90ml (3oz) fiery ginger beer to top

Ice: Crushed

Garnish: Toasted coconut shavings

Equipment: Long bar spoon

Fill a frosted beer mug with crushed ice

Add the coconut rum and blue curaçao

Fill with ginger beer

Stir gently to combine

Garnish with a sprinkle of toasted coconut shavings

MADAGASCAR MULE

MADAGASCAR

The divine spice in the Madagascar Mule is the stuff of sacred splendour. Deep rum beats the drum for its beautiful base before vanilla sweetness moves through the middle, a citrus whip cracks through the fire of ginger beer and cool crushed ice breaks like a soothing wave. Pure percussive perfection.

37.5ml (1¼oz) Dzama Vieux vanilla rum

120ml (4oz) fiery ginger beer to top

¾ of a fresh lime, cut into 3 pieces

1 or 2 dashes vanilla bitters

Ice: Crushed

Equipment: Muddler, long bar spoon

Muddle the lime pieces in a mule cup

Pour in the rum and fill cup with crushed ice

Dash over the bitters and top with ginger beer

Churn gently with a bar spoon to combine

Cap with crushed ice

DOM PEDRO

Legend has it that the Dom Pedro was created by a South African chef who, after visiting Scottish whisky distilleries, decided to soak his ice cream in hooch. You can use the spirit of your choice, here I've deployed brandy for a bit of a change; it can also work splendidly with rum if you feel like shaking things up. Be bold, pick your chosen spirit and infuse away, because this grown-up milkshake is all the pudding you'll ever need. And if you swirl a little chocolate sauce around the inside of the glass before you pour, you win full wow points!

30ml (1oz) Amarula cream liqueur

30ml (1oz) brandy

2 scoops vanilla ice cream

Ice: Crushed

Garnish: Chocolate shavings

Equipment: Blender

Add all the ingredients to a blender cup with half a scoop of crushed ice

Blend on high until you have a smooth, thick cocktail

Tap out into a wine glass

Garnish with a light sprinkling of chocolate shavings

ANSE COCOS

Anse Cocos in the Seychelles is pretty much the ultimate tropical beach – gleaming sands, frilly turquoise ocean and the deep green fringe of the island kissing the shoreline. This cocktail is designed to conjure the same relaxing vibe as that vivid, special place with its exotic rum and sunny ginger spice. Whatever the weather, take your tastebuds direct to the spirit of Anse Coco beach in liquid form.

45ml (1½oz) Takamaka Koko coconut rum

15ml (½oz) Grand Marnier orange liqueur

120ml (4oz) fiery ginger beer to top

2 dashes Angostura bitters

1 orange slice and 1 pineapple slice

Ice: Crushed

Garnish: Orange slice

Equipment: Muddler, long bar spoon

Muddle the orange, pineapple and Angostura bitters in the bottom of a collins glass

Three-quarters fill the glass with crushed ice

Add the coconut rum and Grand Marnier

Top with ginger beer

Churn gently with a bar spoon to combine and cap with crushed ice

Garnish with a slice of orange

THE FYNBOS

SOUTH AFRICA

Fynbos is the name for the biodiverse, scrubby plants and bushes that grow right across the Western Cape. According to the World Wildlife Fund, 'South Africa's Western Cape is more botanically diverse than the richest tropical rainforest in South America, including the Amazon.' With some parts of the fynbos listed as a Unesco World Heritage Site, this cocktail should always to be raised to the magnificence of this treasured ecosystem. Featuring the mellow earthiness of local rooibos tea, it's an all-rounder that works brilliantly in summer as an aromatic quencher or in winter with its warming ginger. Let the toast be 'Fynbos forever!'

45ml (1½oz) brandy

45ml (1½oz) rooibos tea

22.5ml (¾oz) simple syrup (see page 12)

15ml (½oz) Oude Meester ginger liqueur

Dash of Angostura bitters

Ice: Cubed

Garnish: Lemon twist

Equipment: Cocktail shaker, strainer

Brew the rooibos tea as recommended

Fill a cocktail shaker with ice

Add all the ingredients

Shake vigorously to combine and chill

Pour into a chilled cocktail or coupe glass

Garnish with a twist of lemon

A NIGHT IN TUNISIA

TUNISIA

Absinthe delivers the same inspirational boost to the tastebuds as the sound of Dizzy Gillespie's exuberant trumpet does to the ear. The jazz legend wrote the expansive 'A Night in Tunisia' and this cocktail plays homage to that same spirit of wandering wonder. Powerful liquids soar like the sax and trumpet of the song, lifting the sky of the mind to a new dimension. Dizzy would be proud. And he would also remind you that the usual safety warning applies when setting light to drinks.

WATCH THOSE EYEBROWS!

45ml (1½oz) vodka

15ml (½oz) sweet vermouth

15ml (½oz) apricot liqueur

7.5ml (¼oz) absinthe

22.5ml (¾oz) freshly squeezed orange juice

15ml (½oz) freshly squeezed pink grapefruit juice

Ice: Cubed

Garnish: Twist of orange and ground cinnamon

Equipment: Cocktail shaker, strainer, lighter

Fill a cocktail shaker with ice

Add all the ingredients except the absinthe

Shake vigorously to combine and chill

Strain into a chilled cocktail or coupe glass

Gently float the absinthe on top and set it alight

Garnish by squeezing a twist of orange over a flame and then adding a dash of cinnamon

AFRICAN OBSESSION COCKTAIL

SOUTH AFRICA

I've made it to two but never to three of these glossy, silken sensations, such is their satisfying nature. Chocolatey, nutty and lifted by the caramel-citrus influence of the marula fruit, this cocktail is easy to become obsessed with. A lavish treat, it's a destination drink to plan and prepare for – especially if you're listening to the very smoothest of jazz. My top choice to surf the stereo is 'Sunlight' by the Pat Metheny Group, which you can find on the remarkable album *Secret Story*. I double dare you to find the track, pair it with the cocktail and pretend you're mingling with the twinkling lights and endless canapés at my secret pool party. You're 100 per cent invited.

22.5ml (¾oz) Amarula cream liqueur

22.5ml (¾oz) crème de cacao

22.5ml (¾oz) amaretto almond liqueur

45ml (1½oz) single cream

Ice: Cubed

Garnish: Chocolate shavings

Equipment: Cocktail shaker, strainer

Fill a cocktail shaker with ice

Add all the ingredients

Shake vigorously to combine and chill

Strain into a chilled cocktail or coupe glass

Garnish with a light sprinkling of chocolate shavings

MALAWI SHANDY

(NON-ALCOHOLIC)

MALAWI

Part of the Malawi Shandy's allure is the pink tint from the Angostura bitters. It looks like someone has tossed the setting sun into the air and it's miraculously landed in your drink. Sweetly spicy, it's a song of a drink: harmonious, memorable and great for creating an even better mood.

60ml (2oz) lemonade

60ml (2oz) fiery ginger beer

2 dashes Angostura bitters

Ice: Cubed

Garnish: Lime wedge

Equipment: Long bar spoon

Fill a collins glass with ice

Add both lemonade and ginger beer to fill the glass

Dash over the bitters

Stir gently to combine

Garnish with a wedge of lime

For a variant, try the **Rock Shandy** from South Africa, which is equal parts soda water and lemonade topped up with a dash or two of Angostura bitters. Joyful all round.

ZOBO (HIBISCUS) MARTINI

NIGERIA

Zobo, also known as hibiscus, is famous in Nigerian drinks culture and you can use it in loads of cocktails – try a few drops in your next Nigerian Chapman (see page 28) or add it to a Margarita for a flash of colour and a fruitier feel. In this martini it works a charm with the sweet orange of Grand Marnier and the sharper surge of freshly squeezed lime. For eyeball appeal it's hard not to fall in love with Zobo's vivid, purply-pink intensity – and as for its rumoured qualities as an aphrodisiac, all I'll say is that the downright deliciousness of the Zobo Martini makes it perfect for date night.

60ml (2oz) vodka

15ml (½oz) Grand Marnier orange liqueur

22.5ml (¾oz) hibiscus syrup

15ml (½oz) freshly squeezed lime juice

Ice: Cubed

Garnish: Edible flowers

Equipment: Cocktail shaker, strainer

Fill a cocktail shaker with ice

Add all the ingredients and shake hard to combine and chill

Strain into a chilled cocktail or coupe glass

Garnish with a hibiscus flower or any other edible flower

PALM WINE FOREVER

GHANA

Palm wine is created from the sap of a variety of different palms including date and coconut. With its natural sweetness, it's brilliant for boosting fruitiness in cocktails. Alcohol levels can vary, but if you find one at the lower end (no more than 4%), this drink becomes an all-day delight for batch making and basking in the sweetness of an endless summer.

120ml (6oz) palm wine

A large handful of your favourite soft fruit (mango or nectarine work well)

Ice: Crushed

Equipment: Muddler, long bar spoon

Muddle the fruit in a large wine glass

Add the ice and top with palm wine

Stir gently before serving

MANGO COLADA

(NON-ALCOHOLIC)

MAURITIUS

Booze-free cocktails can be spectacular and this one is fruity fireworks. Fresh and creamy, it's a deluxe treat that celebrates Mauritian tropical fruit while making like a modern classic and brightening up any rainy day. Send your spirit on holiday!

60ml (2oz) cream of coconut

30ml (1oz) freshly squeezed pineapple juice

15ml (½oz) freshly squeezed lime juice

60ml (2oz) mango purée or 60g (2oz) frozen mango

Ice: Crushed (if using purée, none if using frozen fruit)

Garnish: Mango slice and pineapple leaf

Equipment: Blender

Add all the ingredients to a blender cup with 1 scoop of crushed ice if using purée

Blend on high until you have a smooth, thick cocktail

Pour into a hurricane glass

Garnish with a slice of fresh or dehydrated mango and a pineapple leaf

MOROCCAN MINT ORANGE JULEP

MOROCCO

Orange and mint synchronize like the hour and minute hand on a cocktail clock. With upbeat orange syrup propelling every flavour forward and the soaring cool trail of mint's lingering freshness, this is the drink that stops time and measures only joy. Moroccan mint is of course a potent symbol of hospitality, and on my first visit to the country a local insisted I visit his home for a restorative mint tea beneath the orange trees in his courtyard. I spent many happy days exploring, inspired by this spontaneous and rather touching hospitality: a timeless gesture that's lingered my whole life long.

75ml (2½oz) bourbon

15ml (½oz) orange syrup

10–12 Moroccan mint leaves

2 dashes orange bitters

Ice: Crushed

Garnish: Mint sprig

Equipment: Muddler, long bar spoon

Muddle the Moroccan mint leaves in a julep cup

Add all the remaining ingredients and fill with crushed ice

Churn gently with a bar spoon to combine and chill

Cap with crushed ice

Garnish with a sprig of mint

Asia

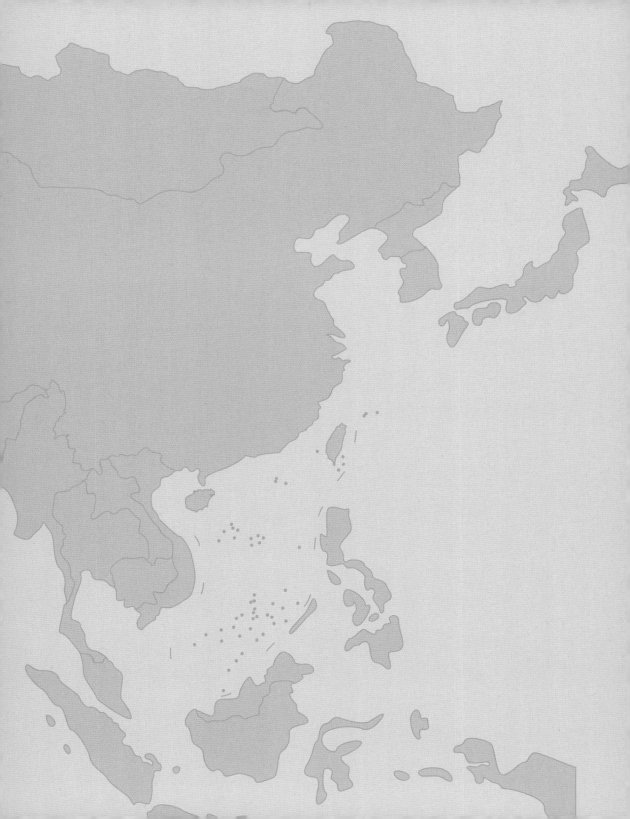

GREEN DRAGON

CHINA

Harking back to one of my favourite musical eras – disco – my take on the Green Dragon is so upbeat it will have you crooning the Bee Gees in no time. Gin and crème de menthe may not instantly appear to jive, but with the mighty herbal bridge built from kümmel's caraway power, their harmony is nothing short of radical. Freak out!

60ml (2oz) gin

15ml (½oz) green crème de menthe

15ml (½oz) kümmel

15ml (½oz) freshly squeezed lemon juice

3 dashes peach bitters

Ice: Cubed

Garnish: Mint sprig

Equipment: Cocktail shaker, strainer

Fill a cocktail shaker with ice

Add all the ingredients

Shake vigorously to combine and chill

Strain into a chilled cocktail or coupe glass

Garnish with a sprig of mint

HONG KONG PEARL

HONG KONG (CHINA – SPECIAL ADMINISTRATIVE REGION)

The Hong Kong Pearl is a powerful potion never to be underestimated. With a nod to the Pearl River Delta (and a certain cocktail named after a cartoon dog voiced by Scatman Crothers), this drink is quite simply as epic as an endless ocean of intrigue. It's the cocktail world's answer to *The Avengers* – a heroic assembly in the name of maximum entertainment for your tastebuds. It's already a blockbuster, but if you really want the double-bill effect, swap out the soda for champagne as an alternative. Kapow!

15ml (½oz) vodka

15ml (½oz) gin

15ml (½oz) white rum

15ml (½oz) tequila

15ml (½oz) Midori melon liqueur

7.5ml (¼oz) absinthe

7.5ml (¼oz) freshly squeezed lemon juice

7.5ml (¼oz) Rose's Lime Juice Cordial

Lemon-lime soda to top

Ice: Cubed

Garnish: Lemon wedge, lime wedge and cocktail cherry

Equipment: Cocktail shaker, strainer

Fill a cocktail shaker with ice

Add all the ingredients except the lemon-lime soda

Shake vigorously to combine and chill

Strain into a collins glass filled with ice

Top with lemon-lime soda

Garnish with wedges of lemon and lime and a speared cherry

SAKE SURGE

If you're fan of the Moscow Mule, you'll adore the Sake Surge. At first, the Sake Surge strikes like citrus lightning, but wait for the swelling, nuanced, savoury depth to spread out like a magic map from your palate to the end of time.

22.5ml (¾oz) sake

22.5ml (¾oz) vodka

22.5ml (¾oz) freshly squeezed yuzu juice (from roughly 1 whole fruit)

Drop of Japanese yuzu bitters (optional)

Fiery ginger beer to top

Ice: Crushed

Garnish: Yuzu slice or lime slice

Equipment: Long bar spoon

Three-quarters fill a mule cup with crushed ice

Add all the ingredients except the ginger beer

Churn gently with a bar spoon

Top with ginger beer and cap with crushed ice

Garnish with a slice of yuzu or lime

Freshly squeezed yuzu is the epitome of awesomeness (but you can buy yuzu juice in certain supermarkets and specialist shops). If not available, substitute with equal parts fresh lemon, lime and grapefruit juice (7.5ml (¼oz) each).

TOKYO MARY

JAPAN

If you want to kickstart your brunch and up the heat in this Tokyo Mary, then wasabi can be added in liberal quantities. Personally I love the pickled ginger twist to bring together the sake and mirin rice wine, just as the recipe stands. But sometimes, the spark plugs of spice are ideal to resurrect the senses from the darkest recesses of the morning after the night before!

45ml (1½oz) sake

7.5ml (¼oz) mirin or sherry

120ml (4oz) tomato or V8 juice

15ml (½oz) freshly squeezed lime juice

7.5ml (¼oz) pickled sushi ginger liquid

2 dashes Worcestershire sauce or soy sauce

A pinch of celery salt and cracked black pepper

½ tsp wasabi (optional)

Ice: Cubed

Garnish: Lime wedge and sushi ginger (optional)

Equipment: Long bar spoon

Fill a collins glass with ice

Add all the ingredients

Stir gently to combine and chill

Garnish with a wedge of lime and a few slivers of sushi ginger, if using

SOJU YOGURT COCKTAIL

SOUTH KOREA

I know, I know, but until you've tasted it, you'll never believe it. This cocktail is massively popular in South Korea and beyond, and it's well worth sticking your yogurt drink in the freezer for up to an hour to bring it down to temperature before you stir up this extraordinary, striking and unique cocktail. Whether you decide to go with ginger ale or lemon-lime soda, just remember to throw in some tasty Korean nibbles on the side too!

60ml (2oz) soju

90ml (3oz) plain yogurt drink (if you don't have access to a Korean yogurt drink you can use Yakult or similar)

Ginger ale or lemon-lime soda, to top

Ice: Cubed

Equipment: Long bar spoon

Fill a highball glass with ice

Add the soju and yogurt drink

Stir gently to combine

Top with the flavoured soda of your choice to taste, then gently stir

THAI PUNCH

THAILAND

A simple fruity punch that is easy to upsize into batches. Thailand is famously home to Ko Khao Phing Kan, a.k.a. James Bond Island, where *The Man with the Golden Gun* was filmed. With a glass of this in hand, unleash the suaveness of my old friend Sir Roger Moore and let the exotic adventure come to you. Eyebrow raising is optional.

45ml (1½oz) Mekhong Thai spirit

15ml (½oz) crème de cassis

45ml (1½oz) freshly squeezed pineapple juice

7.5ml (¼oz) freshly squeezed lime juice

Ice: Cubed

Garnish: Lemon wedge

Equipment: Cocktail shaker, strainer

Fill a cocktail shaker with ice

Add all the ingredients

Shake vigorously to combine and chill

Strain into an old fashioned glass filled with ice

Garnish with a wedge of lemon

SAKE SIDECAR

JAPAN

The classic Sidecar with cognac, triple sec and lemon juice is gorgeous, but subbing sake out for cognac takes the drink to another dimension. The generous serving of sake is key to this drink, and a daiginjo or ginjo are beautifully bright choices to create a riot of refreshment along with that compelling streak of elegant umami. What a drink, what a day, what a chance. Seize it all!

75ml (2½oz) sake

22.5ml (¾oz) Cointreau orange liqueur

22.5ml (¾oz) freshly squeezed lemon juice

Ice: Cubed

Garnish: Lemon twist and orange twist

Equipment: Cocktail shaker, strainer

Fill a cocktail shaker with ice

Add all the ingredients

Shake vigorously to combine and chill

Strain into a chilled coupe glass

Garnish with a twist of lemon and a twist of orange

JUNGLE BIRD

MALAYSIA

Malaysia has given the world many great gifts – two of my favourites are the understated hilarity of comedian Phil Wang and this brilliant cocktail. According to drinks lore, the Jungle Bird was created by Jeffrey Ong for the Hilton Kuala Lumpur's grand opening in 1973. Bittersweet and brilliant, this tremendous tiki homage was served in various vessels in the Aviary Bar, which sadly is no longer there. The spirit of this drink lives on forever in your very next glass and garnish. It echoes the outline of a bird taking wing and shows my gratitude for this cocktail – and for Phil Wang.

45ml (1½oz) Blackstrap dark rum

22.5ml (¾oz) Campari

45ml (1½oz) freshly squeezed pineapple juice

15ml (½oz) freshly squeezed lime juice

7.5ml (¼oz) demerara syrup (see page 13)

Ice: Cubed and crushed

Garnish: Pineapple wedge and leaf

Equipment: Cocktail shaker, strainer

Fill a cocktail shaker with ice

Add all the ingredients

Shake vigorously to combine and chill

Strain into an old fashioned glass filled with crushed ice

Garnish with a pineapple wedge and leaf

MALDIVIAN STINGRAY

MALDIVES

The musical equivalent of this cocktail is the incongruous yet compelling sound of Maldivian singer Sameeu's 'Annaashey Dhaan'. This anthem of my Veligandu honeymoon played daily – it's on the album *Zeeli* if you fancy tracking it down. It even seemed to get trapped in my snorkel, burbling away as I hummed it out loud while trying not to be eaten alive by imaginary sea beasts. For our tenth wedding anniversary I managed to find the track, and it's now the ringtone on Sophie's phone several decades later. If you'd have told me that sipping a creamy coffee cocktail would somehow fit the tropical setting of snow-white beaches and turquoise reefs I'd have giggled; equally, I'd never believe that Maldivian synth-folk would end up being the best ringtone in the galaxy. Cheers!

30ml (1oz) vodka

30ml (1oz) Baileys Irish Cream

30ml (1oz) Tia Maria coffee liqueur

Ice: Cubed

Garnish: Cocktail cherry

Equipment: Cocktail shaker, strainer

Fill a cocktail shaker with ice

Add all the ingredients

Shake vigorously to combine and chill

Strain into a chilled cocktail or coupe glass

Garnish with a speared cocktail cherry

KUMQUAT SOUR

VIETNAM

Kumquat trees are a symbol of prosperity, since they always seem to be laden with fruit. The unmistakable glowing hue and tart shrillness of their bounty always impacts beautifully on a cocktail. Not much bigger than a grape, their enduring appeal is their intensity, sour and tangy – and the skin is one of the more deliciously sweet parts to eat, so make sure you don't throw it away.

60ml (2oz) Vietnamese gin

30ml (1oz) freshly squeezed kumquat juice

15ml (½oz) simple syrup (see page 12)

15ml (½oz) egg white

2 dashes orange bitters (optional)

Ice: Cubed

Garnish: Dehydrated kumquat slice

Equipment: Cocktail shaker, strainer

Add all the ingredients to a cocktail shaker (no ice) and dry shake for a good 30 seconds to break down the egg white

Fill the cocktail shaker with ice

Shake vigorously to combine and chill

Strain into a chilled coupe glass

Garnish with a dehydrated slice of kumquat

As an alternative, you could always make this with clementine juice.

MATCHA MINTY JULEP

JAPAN

The riddle of matcha is tucked into how it manages to be equally serene and energizing. It's a reflective drink: the leaves are grown in the shade to enhance both chlorophyll and colour, and it famously appears as part of the Japanese chanoyu, or tea ceremony, which is laced with Zen Buddhist harmony and mythology. The vivid complexity of green tea in its powdered form lends a bright kick to the scented freshness of mint for a double twist of herbal intrigue. Close your eyes and focus on the next sip. Is it here?

75ml (2½oz) bourbon

10–12 mint leaves

15ml (½oz) demerara syrup (see page 13)

1 tsp matcha powder

Ice: Crushed

Garnish: Mint sprig

Equipment: Muddler, long bar spoon

Muddle the mint leaves and matcha powder in a julep cup

Add all the remaining ingredients and fill with crushed ice

Churn gently with a bar spoon to combine and chill

Garnish with a sprig of mint

QUEEN
MANGO
LASSI

INDIA

A mango is not just a mango. It is an emissary of the mango realm. There are numerous types of mango, and as my friend chef Cyrus Todiwala once told me, there are hundreds of varieties in India alone. Wherever the origin of your mighty mango, one thing is always certain: in a lassi like this one, the combination of fruit and yoghurt cools and feels something like calm. However, the conundrum of cardamom, hailed as the queen of spices, leads the mood from serenity into the sublime with a trail of exotic perfume. Enter the mango realm: no passport required.

37.5ml (1¼oz) dark or gold rum

90ml (3oz) fresh mango purée

90ml (3oz) natural yogurt

15ml (½oz) simple syrup (see page 12)

⅓ tsp ground cardamom

Ice: Crushed

Garnish: Crushed pistachio

Equipment: Blender

Add all the ingredients to a blender cup with 1 scoop of crushed ice

Blend on high until you have a smooth, thick cocktail

Tap out into a hurricane glass

Garnish with a light sprinkling of crushed pistachios

For anyone with a nut allergy, a slice of mango instead of pistachios will do just fine.

And for a Virgin Queen Mango Lassi, omit the rum. It's majestic.

MALDIVIAN LADY

MALDIVES

My wife Sophie and I spent our honeymoon in the Maldives on the island of Veligandu, and it was altogether blissful... aside from 'the Buffet of Shame', which we never mention. I've never really grasped the significance of this particular cocktail's name, but in essence it's become the national cocktail of the Maldives. In some ways I wish it was called the Maldivian Dream, because whenever I sip it I seem to be back under those idyllic swaying palms, in no way regretting my choices at that buffet of dreams.

45ml (1½oz) gold rum

22.5ml (¾oz) apricot liqueur

90ml (3oz) freshly squeezed orange juice

90ml (3oz) freshly squeezed pineapple juice

7.5ml (⅓oz) grenadine or grenadine syrup (see page 12)

Ice: Cubed and crushed

Garnish: Wedge and leaf of pineapple and cocktail cherry

Equipment: Cocktail shaker, strainer

Fill a cocktail shaker with ice

Add all the ingredients

Shake vigorously to combine and chill

Strain into a hurricane glass filled with crushed ice

Garnish with a pineapple wedge speared with a cherry on a cocktail stick

YUZU COLLINS

JAPAN

The flavour of a Yuzu Collins is like a mirror held up to the breeze. It's a powerful palate clarifier thanks to the dazzling thrust of yuzu. Don't be fooled if your drink is a touch on the cloudy side – the flavours are as precise as a laser beam leading you to the very centre of stimulation. And if you can't find yuzu, freshly squeezed grapefruit juice is the understudy of choice.

45ml (1½oz) Japanese gin

22.5ml (¾oz) freshly squeezed yuzu juice

7.5ml (¼oz) simple syrup (see page 12)

2 dashes orange bitters

Soda water to top

Ice: Cubed

Garnish: Yuzu slice and leaf

Equipment: Cocktail shaker, strainer

Fill a cocktail shaker with ice

Add all the ingredients except the soda water

Shake vigorously to combine and chill

Strain into a collins glass filled with ice

Top with soda water

Garnish with a slice of yuzu and a yuzu leaf

ARAK MADU

Lebanon is part of western Asia and the Arak Madu is a cocktail with a kick! Arak has deep roots in Levantine culture and is traditionally made from aniseed and grapes (good bottles are often produced by wineries), so you could think of it as a relation of ouzo or pastis. The mysterious compound anethole, found in aniseed, is soluble in alcohol but not water, hence the milkiness when such drinks are mixed with water – my tip is to add ice after you've poured water to avoid solids forming. Sweetened with honey, the Arak Madu is great with mezze or as an early afternoon pick-me-up.

60ml (2oz) arak

22.5ml (¾oz) freshly squeezed lime juice

22.5ml (¾oz) honey

7.5ml (¼oz) chilled water

Ice: Cubed

Garnish: Lime wedge

Equipment: Cocktail shaker, strainer

Fill a cocktail shaker with ice

Add all the ingredients

Shake vigorously to combine and chill

Strain into a chilled cocktail or coupe glass

Garnish with a wedge of lime

TAIPEI SUMMER SOUR

TAIWAN/CHINA

Fermented sorghum from the grass family is the base behind kaoliang liquor, which leads the charge in this fluffy eruption of a cocktail. Scrumptious!

45ml (1½oz) kaoliang liquor

22.5ml (¾oz) St-Germain elderflower liqueur

60ml (2oz) freshly squeezed orange juice

60ml (2oz) freshly squeezed pineapple juice

15ml (½oz) freshly squeezed lemon juice

7.5ml (¼oz) grenadine or grenadine syrup (see page 12)

15ml (½oz) egg white

Ice: Cubed

Garnish: Dehydrated lemon slice

Equipment: Cocktail shaker, strainer

Add all the ingredients to a cocktail shaker without ice and dry shake to break down the egg white

Fill the shaker with ice

Shake vigorously to chill

Strain into a chilled coupe glass

Garnish with a dehydrated slice of lemon

MESTIZA

Three simple ingredients and a staple of the colourful islands of the Philippines, the Mestiza is a drink you can customize to taste according to your mood. Easy to assemble, a great thirst quencher for summer and also a drink with a hidden kick to it. You'll love it!

45ml (1½oz) Filipino rum (Don Papa is widely available, but keep your eye out for Kasama small batch rum)

90ml (3oz) Filipino beer

90ml (3oz) soda (cola or lemon-lime)

Ice: Cubed

Garnish: Lime wedge

Fill a collins glass with ice

Add the rum and top with beer and the soda of your choice

Garnish with a wedge of lime

ARAK BUCK

This gorgeous teatime treat is served all across the Levant. Buck cocktails usually consist of a spirit mixed with citrus and either ginger ale or ginger beer; here it's enhanced with the orange impact of triple sec. As soon as you taste it, this cocktail adopts its unofficial code name... 'Afternoon Delight'.

45ml (1½oz) arak

15ml (½oz) triple sec

15ml (½oz) freshly squeezed lemon juice

90ml (3oz) ginger ale to top

Ice: Cubed

Garnish: Lemon wedge

Equipment: Long bar spoon

Fill a collins glass with ice

Add all the ingredients except the ginger ale

Stir gently to combine and chill

Top with ginger ale and stir once more

Garnish with a wedge of lemon

SOJU ORANGE SEOUL

SOUTH KOREA

Soju is traditionally a clear, neutral South Korean spirit usually distilled from rice, potatoes or grains. As I type this, Jinro soju is the best-selling spirit brand worldwide by volume. Jinro 24, bottled at 24% ABV, is a good bet for making soju cocktails. If you're interested in tasting soju neat, Sulseam Mir soju (22%) is delightfully pure, and made from rice, water and nuruk (a traditional Korean fermenter starter) – and it also makes a thrillingly fresh and luxuriant Soju Orange Seoul. (See also the **Soju Yogurt Cocktail** on page 60.)

60ml (2oz) soju

½ an orange, cut into eighths

15ml (½oz) sugar syrup

7.5ml (¼oz) freshly squeezed lime juice

Ice: Crushed

Garnish: Dehydrated orange slice

Equipment: Long bar spoon

Muddle the orange pieces in the bottom of an old fashioned glass

Three-quarters fill the glass with crushed ice

Add the remaining ingredients, stir and churn with a bar spoon to combine

Cap with crushed ice

Garnish with a dehydrated slice of orange

COCONUT KISS

My favourite of all the Maldives' fabulous bounty is the coconut. The silhouette and sound of the palms themselves are iconic – I can picture them now with a purple-bronze sunset folding into the inky skies above them. I salute the coconut's many contributions to human life: it provides materials for mats, ropes, baskets, buildings, boats and thatching; refreshing coconut water; and perhaps most memorable of all, the pale, rich, creamy flesh. When a coconut falls from above, it is the heaviest and most welcome blessing on the beach. And this luxuriant tropical cocktail is the perfect glass to raise in reverence.

45ml (1½oz) freshly squeezed passionfruit juice

45ml (1½oz) cherry juice

30ml (1oz) coconut water

22.5ml (¾oz) cream of coconut

Dash of grenadine or grenadine syrup (see page 12)

Ice: Cubed and crushed

Garnish: Pineapple wedge

Equipment: Cocktail shaker, strainer

Fill a cocktail shaker with ice

Add all the ingredients

Shake vigorously to combine and chill

Strain into a hurricane glass filled with crushed ice

Garnish with a pineapple wedge

SHOCHU HIGHBALL

(CHUHAI)

JAPAN

Behold the Shochu Highball, the fruity sparkling karaoke classic to loosen your vocal cords. Shochu is a clear spirit with a subtle flavour and an alcohol level usually around 20–30%, which makes it a handy alternative to spirits over 40% such as vodka. In Japan, shochu is a national treasure of a drink, and you can customize it with any fruit juice that takes your fancy. Cans of chuhai or shochu cocktails like this one are widely available across Japan from kiosks and vending machines, and it's a delightfully simple cocktail to make for yourself. While good-value shochu is fine for this fruity mix, I prefer shopping around for a decent quality bottle, which you could also try sipping neat with a little ice or a splash of water. The range of starchy bases that lead to shochu are numerous, from rice and barley to sweet potatoes and brown sugar, so finding the one you love most is well worth doing. Kitaya is a good name to look out for, or if you can find it, Mizuho Shuzo produces excellent shochu from Okinawa. Since shochu is the most popular spirit in Japan, each iteration offers alluring intrigue.

45ml (1½oz) shochu

45ml (1½oz) fruit juice (strawberry, raspberry, apple, peach or yuzu)

90ml (3oz) soda water to top

Ice: Cubed

Garnish: Fruit of your choice

Equipment: Cocktail shaker, strainer

Fill a cocktail shaker with ice

Add all the ingredients except the soda water

Shake vigorously to combine and chill

Strain into a highball glass filled with ice

Top with soda

Garnish with your speared fruit of choice

OLLY'S SHOCHU HIGHBALL

(CHUHAI)

JAPAN

I fell in love with lychees through my secret childhood passion for Turkish Delight. I find the super-scented, hedonistic exoticism of lychees irresistible. When zinging yuzu and fragrant cherry blossom syrup twirl together and the flavours start to boogie, I can practically hear 'Welcome to the Pleasuredome' by Frankie Goes To Hollywood rolling towards my ears on a distant breeze. The extended version of that track is one of my all-time favourite tunes, and indeed the first record that I ever bought. I warmly recommend cranking it up to the maximum level your stereo can pump while sipping my Shochu Highball and dancing with delight!

45ml (1½oz) shochu

15ml (½oz) lychee juice

22.5ml (¾oz) freshly squeezed yuzu juice

7.5ml (¼oz) cherry blossom syrup

Soda water to top

Ice: Cubed

Garnish: Lychees

Equipment: Cocktail shaker, strainer

Fill a cocktail shaker with ice

Add all the ingredients except the soda water

Shake vigorously to combine and chill

Strain into a highball glass filled with ice

Top with soda

Garnish with 2 speared lychees

MUMBAI MULE

INDIA

The first time I tasted a Mumbai Mule was with Michelin-starred chef Atul Kochhar – his recipe rocked my world! The gingery spice is a headline of happiness and is pitch perfect to quench, invigorate and build a surging thirst for the next sip. Behold the cyclical magic of the Mumbai Mule... where one is made, two will follow!

45ml (1½oz) vodka

22.5ml (¾oz) freshly squeezed lime juice

7.5ml (¼oz) spiced ginger syrup (see page 13)

Fiery ginger beer to top

Ice: Crushed

Garnish: Lime wedge

Equipment: Long bar spoon

Three-quarters fill a mule cup with crushed ice

Add all the ingredients except the ginger beer

Churn gently with a bar spoon

Top with ginger beer and cap with crushed ice

Garnish with a wedge of lime

BORACAY

PHILIPPINES

Tanduay and Emperador are both big local brands in the Philippines, and if you're a fan of an Espresso Martini or a White Russian, you'll adore this Boracay. Just make sure you give it a good shake to ensure a silky-smooth finish. It's so dreamy that it may even conjure memories you never knew you had of Boracay island and some of the world's most beautiful beaches.

45ml (1½oz) Tanduay rum (Emperador brandy can also be used)

90ml (3oz) freshly brewed espresso coffee, chilled

15ml (½oz) condensed milk

2 tsp chocolate malt powder

Ice: Cubed

Equipment: Cocktail shaker, strainer

Fill a cocktail shaker with ice

Add all the ingredients

Shake vigorously to combine and chill

Strain into a highball glass filled with ice

BANDREK

(NON-ALCOHOLIC)

I love Indonesia, a magical archipelago wreathed in fragrant spices. I lived there a long time ago in a previous life working as an English teacher at the University of Jambi, Sumatra. Strolling solo across the islands on a journey of many months, I picked wild cinnamon bark from trees, inhaled the sweet smoke of sugary cloves from scented kretek cigarettes and discovered the many dimensions of flavour within spices. It's a whole library of itself with indexes of intensity and a multitude of approaches to teasing out combinations of splendour. Bandrek is one of the most beautifully warming drinks in the world, and if you want to play around with the flavours, peppercorns, cardamom pods and fresh chillies can all bring spectacular dimensions of additional heat. Adding coconut flesh is also a lovely way of serving the drink too. And if you ever get the chance, visit these wonderful islands and explore the dreamy diversity of dishes for yourself. Indonesia keeps some of the greatest secrets of the spice world and I'd love you to share in them.

454ml (16oz) water

2 pandan leaves (simply omit if you can't find them)

Fresh root ginger (approx 25g/¾oz)

1 cinnamon stick

2 lemongrass stalks

1 star anise

4 cloves

2 tbsp palm sugar (brown sugar works if you can't find palm)

30ml (1oz) condensed milk or coconut milk

Garnish: Pandan leaf

Equipment: Saucepan, muddler, strainer

Put the water in a pan and bring to the boil then reduce to a simmer

Slice the ginger and pandan leaves into large slivers

Gently bruise the remaining herbs and spices with a muddler

Add everything except the sugar and condensed milk to the water and gently simmer for 20 minutes

Add the palm sugar and stir until dissolved

Remove from the heat, cover and leave to steep for 15 minutes

Strain into two warmed serving mugs, then add the condensed milk to your desired taste

Garnish with a pandan leaf

CUCUMBER SAKETINI

JAPAN

Lisa Ball is credited with creating the original Saketini in London in 2004. In this recipe, the quantities nudge in vodka's favour, which works especially well with a light, fragrant daiginjo sake. Perfect refreshment for mellow summer sipping, whatever the weather!

60ml (2oz) vodka

30ml (1oz) sake

7.5ml (¼oz) simple syrup (see page 12)

2.5cm (1in) cucumber, cut into small cubes

Ice: Cubed

Garnish: Cucumber curl

Equipment: Mixing glass, muddler, long bar spoon, strainer

Muddle the cucumber in the bottom of a mixing glass

Fill with ice and add the remaining ingredients

Stir gently to combine and chill

Strain into a chilled cocktail or coupe glass

Garnish with a curl of cucumber (use a peeler to peel along the length of a cucumber and curl it into the glass – you can fix it with a cocktail stick if that's easier)

SABAI SABAI

If you're a Collins drinker, the Sabai Sabai is going to be right up your street. It's as fresh and exhilarating as sky-diving into a lake bobbing with lemons – and just get your chops around the complexity of those aromatic Thai basil leaves for a face-blast of fragrance.

45ml (1½oz) Mekhong Thai spirit

30ml (1oz) freshly squeezed lemon juice

22.5ml (¾oz) simple syrup (see page 12)

3 or 4 Thai basil leaves

Soda water to top

Ice: Cubed

Garnish: Thai basil sprig

Equipment: Cocktail shaker, strainer

Fill a cocktail shaker with ice

Add all the ingredients except the soda water

Shake vigorously to combine and chill

Strain into an old fashioned glass filled with ice

Top with soda water

Garnish with a small sprig of Thai basil

CHINA
BLUE

JAPAN

In spite of its name, the China Blue is thought to have emerged from Japan in the 1990s. These days, however, it is sipped across East Asia and far beyond. It's as eyecatching as it is scrumptious, turquoise as it is tantalizing. And thanks to the electrifying jolt of pink grapefruit, it's far zingier than you might imagine, which makes it spot-on for brunch. In fact, it's a contender for any spontaneous celebration thanks to its dazzling hue and striking simplicity. No time to lose: time to go blue.

30ml (1oz) lychee liqueur

30ml (1oz) blue curaçao

120ml (4oz) freshly squeezed pink grapefruit juice

Ice: Cubed

Garnish: Orange slice and lychee

Equipment: Cocktail shaker, strainer

Fill a cocktail shaker with ice

Add all the ingredients

Shake vigorously to combine and chill

Strain into a collins glass filled with ice

Garnish with an orange slice and a speared lychee

SINGAPORE SLING

(RAFFLES RECIPE)

SINGAPORE

A big ripple in this breaking wave of a cocktail is Bénédictine. Somehow it never finds a final beach to cascade onto, though, and the Singapore Sling rolls effortlessly through the years. It's inextricably linked to the Raffles Hotel in Singapore, which was occupied in 1942 by Japan and subsequently used by the Allies to shift prisoners of war in 1945: its history is extraordinary.

30ml (1oz) gin

15ml (½oz) Heering cherry liqueur

7.5ml (¼oz) Bénédictine

7.5ml (¼oz) Cointreau orange liqueur

120ml (4oz) freshly squeezed pineapple juice

15ml (½oz) freshly squeezed lime juice

7.5ml (¼oz) grenadine or grenadne syrup (see page 12)

Dash of Angostura bitters

Soda water to top

Ice: Cubed

Garnish: Lemon-cherry flag

Equipment: Cocktail shaker, strainer

Fill a cocktail shaker with ice

Add all the ingredients except the soda water

Shake vigorously to combine and chill

Strain into a sling glass filled with ice

Top with soda water

Garnish with a lemon-cherry flag

VIETNAMESE ICED COFFEE BOBA

(NON-ALCOHOLIC)

VIETNAM

I remember my youngest daughter Lily went through a massive boba phase and my whole family found the bursting mystery of these enchanting pearls utterly baffling. They've proved great fun to play with across a range of flavours, and this recipe delivers fantastic refreshment for warmer weather. Be warned, Vietnamese coffee seems to be far stronger than any I've ever tasted – think of it like an espresso made for a giant. You could always tame it by adding a syrup and recreating your favourite flavoured coffee.

60ml (2oz) freshly brewed Vietnamese coffee, chilled

60ml (2oz) condensed milk

180ml (6oz) water

60g (2oz) tapioca pearls

Honey or vanilla sugar to taste

15ml (½oz) flavoured syrup (optional)

Ice: Cubed

Garnish: Whipped cream

Equipment: Long bar spoon

Cook the tapioca pearls as per instructions and cool under cold water

Place the cooled tapioca pearls in a tall glass and fill with ice

Add the remaining ingredients and stir with a long bar spoon

Garnish with a swirl of whipped cream and a thick boba straw

ASIAN PEAR MULE

CHINA

Asian pears have a crunchy, grainy texture with a scented, exotic tang. This cocktail delivers the same ignition for your appetite. Spicy and zesty, it's a sharpener, a tantalizer and a tribute to the day to come or the day that's done – all in one.

60ml (2oz) pear vodka

Drop of pear bitters (optional)

90ml (3oz) fiery ginger beer

15ml (½oz) freshly squeezed lime juice

Ice: Crushed

Garnish: Slices of Asian pear

Equipment: Long bar spoon

Three-quarters fill a mule cup with crushed ice

Add all the ingredients except the ginger beer

Churn gently with a bar spoon

Top with ginger beer and cap with crushed ice

Garnish with a fan of thinly sliced Asian pear

SCOTCH AND GREEN TEA

CHINA

Tea and whisky are two drinks beloved across the globe, and surprisingly their blending opportunities are remarkable. The mixture of green tea and whisky was a revelation to me on my first visit to Beijing, and I adored it right from the off. Green tea has a herbaceous brightness that works a charm in this recipe – think of it operating in a similar way to a citrus slice in a whisky highball. The spicy sweetness of Scotch is boosted by the simple syrup, creating a halo of happiness floating above their joyful union.

45ml (1½oz) blended Scotch whisky (Chivas Regal or Johnnie Walker Blue Label are popular)

120ml (4oz) green tea, brewed and cooled (avoid over-steeping the tea to keep the flavours fresh rather than bitter)

7.5ml (¼oz) simple syrup (see page 12)

Ice: Large cube

Equipment: Long bar spoon

Place a large ice cube into a rocks glass

Add the ingredients

Stir gently to combine and chill

JAPANESE HIGHBALLL

JAPAN

I've only visited Japan once, yet it left a deep impression on me. To this day, one of my favourite poets is Matsuo Kinsaku, a great haiku poet, who changed his named to Bashō in honour of a rare banana tree given to him by a disciple. Monastic yet a compulsive traveller, Bashō was a master of both precision as well as rule bending, understanding that sometimes imperfection is sacred. Some might say that mixing the splendour of a Japanese whisky is sacrilege; however, this drink is heavenly and the recipe thrives with lighter whiskies such as Nikka Days. Sipping a Japanese Highball alongside reading a ruddy good book typifies the lightness, purity and equanimity of life's most finely balanced pleasures. Drink deep for the spirit!

60ml (2oz) Japanese whisky

90ml (3oz) green tea, brewed and cooled (avoid over-steeping to keep the flavours fresh)

Soda water to top

Ice: Cubed

Garnish: Lemon twist

Equipment: Long bar spoon

Fill a highball glass with ice and add the Japanese whisky and green tea

Top with soda water

Stir gently to combine and chill

Garnish with a twist of lemon

TAMARIND GINGER MARGARITA

INDIA

My friend Marcus from Goa always kindly gives me the greatest tamarind paste whenever we meet, and it's one of my all-time favourite flavours. I love its sour fragrance and use it endlessly in recipes alongside citrus and ginger. While this cocktail may sound mild, the flavours ripple and burst – and that gingery salt rim is a gorgeously tasty glittering constellation!

45ml (1½oz) reposado tequila

22.5ml (¾oz) triple sec

22.5ml (¾oz) freshly squeezed lime juice

15ml (½oz) spiced ginger syrup (see page 13)

7.5ml (¼oz) tamarind paste

Ice: Cubed

Garnish: Salt rim and lime twist

Equipment: Cocktail shaker, strainer

Fill a cocktail shaker with ice

Add all the ingredients

Shake vigorously to combine and chill

Use a little ginger syrup to wet the rim of a cocktail or coupe glass, then dip it in the salt and add the lime twist on the side

Strain into the prepared glass

COLORADO BOBADOG

This bubble-tea take on a Colorado Bulldog celebrates the fun of boba pearls, which also add a touch of sweetness. For a variation you could switch the coffee liqueur for tea liqueur. Either way, the textural impact of black boba pearls is a joy.

30ml (1oz) vanilla vodka

30ml (1oz) Kahlúa coffee liqueur

30ml (1oz) single cream

60ml (2oz) cola

60g (2oz) black boba pearls (quick-cook are the best)

Ice: Cubed

Garnish: Boba straw

Equipment: Cocktail shaker, strainer

Cook boba pearls as per instructions and cool under cold water

Add the pearls to a boba cup or suitable glass

Half-fill the cup with ice

Fill a cocktail shaker with ice and add all the ingredients except the cola and boba pearls

Shake vigorously to combine and chill

Strain into the prepared cup or glass

Serve with a boba straw

BIYADHOO SPECIAL

MALDIVES

The Biyadhoo revels in its simplicity – it makes me feel like I'm riding a melon ball the size of a car into the world's best beach bar. It's a cracking cocktail that deserves greater respect, and it's as quick to make as it is to thrill.

45ml (1½oz) Midori melon liqueur

22.5ml (¾oz) vodka

45ml (1½oz) freshly squeezed pineapple juice

Ice: Cubed and crushed

Garnish: Wedge of pineapple and cocktail cherry

Equipment: Cocktail shaker, strainer

Fill a cocktail shaker with ice

Add all the ingredients

Shake vigorously to combine and chill

Strain into a highball glass filled with crushed ice

Garnish with a pineapple wedge speared with a cherry on a cocktail stick

MILO DE LUXE

(A.K.A. MILO ALEXANDER)

MALAYSIA

Milo is a Malaysian malty chocolate drink that sort of reminds me of Ovaltine (which you could always use here as a substitute if Milo is proving elusive). This luxurious recipe is a go-to indulgence for me in winter – its rich chocolate fluffiness is instantly comforting, like a duvet of delight wrapping itself around you.

45ml (1½oz) cognac

15ml (½oz) dark crème de cacao

15ml (½oz) white crème de cacao

30ml (1oz) single cream

2 tsp Milo chocolate powder (or your favourite powdered chocolate drink)

Ice: Cubed

Garnish: Chocolate powder

Equipment: Cocktail shaker, strainer

Fill a cocktail shaker with ice

Add all the ingredients

Shake vigorously to combine and chill

Strain into a chilled cocktail or coupe glass

Garnish with a light sprinkling of Milo chocolate powder

Europe

TURKISH COSMO

TURKEY

Pomegranates are seen as a symbol of prosperity, good fortune and abundance in Turkey and at weddings, pomegranates are even smashed on the floor with juice given to guests to wish joy to the newlyweds. On December 31st, you could even embrace the tradition of throwing a pomegranate on the doorstep of your home to bid welcome to the New Year. Or just celebrate the ruby jewel-like splendour of their seeds with this fruity cocktail. 'Şerefe!'

60ml (2oz) vodka

15ml (½oz) triple sec

45ml (1½oz) pomegranate juice

15ml (½oz) freshly squeezed lime juice

2 dashes raki

Ice: Cubed

Garnish: Orange twist

Equipment: Cocktail shaker, strainer

Dash raki into a chilled cocktail or coupe glass. Swirl and discard

Add all the remaining ingredients to a cocktail shaker

Shake vigorously to combine and chill

Strain into the chilled cocktail or coupe glass

Garnish with a twist of orange

CHOCOLATE MANHATTAN

UNITED KINGDOM

This recipe was given to me by Charlie, a brilliant barman at Chewton Glen, hotel of glory on the fringes of the New Forest in southern England. In spite of the name, this is very much a bitter and complex drink, one for a serious-minded moment, preferably to be savoured with a square of dark chocolate to nibble on. If you enjoy a dry oloroso sherry, this will be right up your street. Cheers to Chewton Glen, a royal treat of a place to stay, to Charlie for generously sharing the recipe and to you for making it.

60ml (2oz) Irish whiskey

30ml (1oz) Antica Formula

3 dashes chocolate bitters

Ice: Cubed

Garnish: Orange twist

Equipment: Mixing glass, long bar
    spoon, strainer

Fill a mixing glass with ice

Add all the ingredients

Stir gently to combine and chill

Strain into a chilled coupe glass

Garnish with a twist of orange

GLÖGG

SWEDEN

Mugs filled with Glögg are an integral part of a Swedish Christmas. Derived from the old Swedish word 'glödg' or 'glödga', which is linked to warming up, this festival of sweet spice tends to have a bit more complexity than regular mulled wine recipes and if you want to nibble on the soaked fruit and almonds ladled into the bottom of your glass, dive right in! Small glasses are best so that you can keep your glöggfester (glögg party) going as long as possible – stick Abba on loop and embrace the long dark months of perfect excuses to glow from within.

750ml (25oz) red wine

180ml (6oz) aquavit (or a Swedish vodka)

200g (7oz) golden caster sugar

8 cardamom pods

4 cloves

1 cinnamon stick

3 twists of orange

3 slices of ginger root

40g (1½oz) golden raisins

40g (1½oz) slivered almonds

Garnish: Winter fruits

Equipment: Saucepan

Add all the ingredients except the aquavit to a non-reactive saucepan.

Warm gently (do not boil) for about 15 minutes

Add the aquavit (or vodka) and stir gently to combine

Serve warm in glögg mugs

Garnish with seasonal fruits (orange zest, cranberries, pomegranate, etc.)

HANKY PANKY

UNITED KINGDOM

The story goes that this famous variation on a Martini was created in the Savoy's American Bar by Ada 'Coley' Coleman, the first female head bartender in the joint. She'd come up with this new concoction for actor Sir Charles Hawtrey in the early 1900s and apparently when he sipped it for the first time, Hawtrey declared it 'the real hanky panky'. The name stuck, although I sort of wish we could rename it a 'Coley Coleman' since we really ought to be thanking Ada for such a gem of a drink.

45ml (1½oz) gin

45ml (1½oz) sweet red vermouth

2 dashes Fernet-Branca

Dash of freshly squeezed orange juice (optional)

Ice: Cubed

Garnish: Orange twist

Equipment: Mixing glass, long bar spoon, strainer

Fill a mixing glass with ice

Add all the ingredients

Stir gently to combine and chill

Strain into a chilled cocktail or coupe glass

Garnish with a twist of orange

AQUAGRONI

DENMARK

I spent the best part of a year on and off filming in Denmark and I fell in love with the people, open sandwiches and of course, aquavit. 'Skål' – cheers – became a watchword throughout the trip as we sampled traditional aquavit flavoured with dill and caraway. In fact, this water of life inspired many moments in front of the camera executing my speciality of 'talky-talky-word-word'. Aquavit shares its moment equally here with Campari. Friends and those familiar with my recipes will already know of my deep lust for Campari. It possesses my soul. I am Campari. We are Campari. To Campari is to live. Campari has little to do with Denmark but who cares, it's magnificent. Be more Campari.

30ml (1oz) aquavit

30ml (1oz) Campari

30ml (1oz) Cinzano 1757 Rosso

2 dashes orange bitters

Ice: Cubed

Garnish: Dehydrated orange slice

Equipment: Mixing glass, long bar
    spoon, strainer

Fill a mixing glass with ice

Add all the ingredients

Stir gently to combine and chill

Strain into a rocks glass filled with ice

Garnish with a dehydrated slice of orange

KOPSTOOT

NETHERLANDS

No trip to Holland is complete without a Kopstoot and the next best thing is bringing it into your home. Fill your shooter (ideally tulip shaped) with chilled jenever to the brim. Hands behind your back, take your first sip, then pick up your beer and have a sip. From here on you can alternate and use your hands, a surprisingly civilized way to 'headbutt' or kopstoot.

30ml (1oz) chilled jenever

300ml (10oz/½ pint) Belgian ale

Pour the jenever into a chilled shot glass

Pour the ale into a chilled beer glass

AYRAN

(NON-ALCOHOLIC)

TURKEY

I came across this in Çirali on Turkey's southern coast... it was a time of turtles, a lost attempt at a marriage proposal, getting bitten by flying beasts, an injection in the rump, hot fires springing from naked rocks and the local pide – think flatbread coated with all the delicious things in the world. Brilliant to sip alongside spicy food, this drink was a welcome calming balm in the midst of a frenetic trip which helped settled my soul and prepare for the marriage proposal that eventually came, albeit several months later. For a frothier drink in celebration of such a happy event as marriage, use sparkling water instead of still.

300ml (10oz) plain yogurt

210ml (7oz) chilled water

Pinch of salt

Optional flavourings: 10 mint leaves / 4 slices cucumber / pinch of cracked pepper

Ice: Crushed

Equipment: Blender

Add all the ingredients to a blender cup with 1 scoop of crushed ice

Add the flavouring of your choice, should you wish

Blend on high until well mixed and a little frothy

Tap out into a chilled collins glass

CALIMOCHO

SPAIN

This is a super-simple but very traditional drink that I first tasted one morning in the Basque Country. It may seem like lunacy but I'd popped over for lunch with leading British chef Chris Mackett to dine in the famous Asador Etxebarri restaurant in Axpe with its notoriously scarce availability. Lunch was exceptional and Chris is always one of my favourite people to share a table with. The very first time I presented *Saturday Kitchen* on BBC1 I went for lunch afterwards with Chris and my family to Theo Randall at the InterContinental in London, as he brings every moment to life with his astute commentary. Back in the Basque Country that legendary day before lunch, Chris and I were presented with the local Calimocho, a.k.a. Kalimotxo – a mix of red wine with cola – in a tiny bar nearby. After exchanging quizzical glances, we dived in. It was surprisingly good, a perfectly serviceable party drink; no need to splash out on a top vintage, just use young, fruity, cheap and cheerful red wine. And if you can follow it with the feast of your dreams, so much the better.

90ml (3oz) Spanish red wine (a rioja joven is ideal)

90ml (3oz) cola

Ice: Cubed

Equipment: Long bar spoon

Fill a collins glass with ice

Add all the ingredients

Stir gently to combine and chill

ROSEMARY DRAMBLE

UNITED KINGDOM

A variation on the Dramble, which itself is a variation on the Bramble, my Rosemary Dramble has that citrus-lavender-sage woody effect that this common but special herb delivers. I wore rosemary on my wedding day as my 'garnish' – it's known as a symbol of remembrance, and as Shakespeare's Ophelia hands out flowers and herbs she says: 'There's rosemary, that's for remembrance.' An apt cocktail to raise to absent friends.

45ml (1½oz) blended Scotch whisky

15ml (½oz) crème de mûre

22.5ml (¾oz) freshly squeezed lemon juice

15ml (½oz) rosemary syrup (see page 15)

Ice: Crushed

Garnish: Blackberry and a small rosemary sprig

Equipment: Long bar spoon

Three-quarters fill an old fashioned glass with crushed ice

Add the Scotch, lemon juice and rosemary syrup

Churn with a bar spoon to chill and combine

Cap with a little more crushed ice and drizzle the crème de mûre on top

Garnish with a single blackberry and a sprig of fresh rosemary

MALTESE BAJTRA SPRITZ

MALTA

For some reason at home we use the term 'Maltese Pantomime' to denote anything connected with chaos and lust. 'How did the meeting go?' 'Started well but ended down the pub in a ruddy Maltese Pantomime!' I love Malta, so I have no idea how we coined this particular phrase but the Maltese Bajtra Spritz is far more salubrious and indeed delicious. Made from local prickly pears, Bajtra is uniquely Maltese and this drink is a must-taste for anyone who's ever enjoyed an Aperol Spritz. You never know, it may lead to an actual Maltese Pantomime!

60ml (2oz) Bajtra prickly pear cactus liqueur

90ml (3oz) Maltese sparkling wine (or prosecco)

15ml (½oz) freshly squeezed lemon juice

30ml (1oz) soda water to top

Ice: Cubed

Garnish: Lemon twist

Equipment: Long bar spoon

Fill a collins glass with ice

Add the Bajtra and lemon juice, stir once

Add the Maltese sparkling wine and soda water

Stir once to combine

Garnish with a twist of lemon

REVEREND HUBERT'S BLESSING

UNITED KINGDOM

Reverend Hubert Summer Cup, a fruity gin liqueur, is made in the Cotswolds and inspired by a recipe from founder Thomas Lester's great grandfather, the Reverend Hubert Bell Lester, who fashioned such drinks for his congregation. This liqueur is legendary, bursting with lush plum, ripe pomegranates, zingy rhubarb and tangy cranberries – perfect for invoking a vicarage garden in full bloom. It's a summer staple in my life and a great way to showcase the bright fizz of English sparking wine too. Bravo to Thomas and Joe, the team who brought Reverend Hubert's blessings back to the world.

45ml (1½oz) Reverend Hubert Summer Cup

15ml (½oz) St-Germain elderflower liqueur

90ml (3oz) English sparkling wine to top

30ml (1oz) ginger ale to top

Ice: Cubed

Garnish: Strawberry

Equipment: Long bar spoon

Fill a collins glass with ice

Add all the ingredients except the sparkling wine and the ginger ale

Stir once to combine

Gently pour in the sparkling wine and ginger ale and stir once more

Garnish with a ripe summer strawberry

IRISH BLACKTHORN

Warning! This is an incredibly dry cocktail dating back to the early 1900s and features in the famous *Savoy Cocktail Book*. For a gentler outing, use half dry and half sweet vermouth, 22.5ml (½oz) of each (known as 'perfect'). The wood from a blackthorn is used for creating the multipurpose walking stick/cudgel known in Ireland as a shillelagh sometimes used to settle disagreements. So make sure before you start making this cocktail that you agree on whether you're going dry or perfect!

45ml (1½oz) Irish whiskey

45ml (1½oz) dry vermouth

3 dashes absinthe

3 dashes Angostura bitters

Ice: Cubed

Garnish: Lemon twist

Equipment: Mixing glass, long bar spoon, strainer

Fill a mixing glass with ice

Add all the ingredients

Stir gently to combine and chill

Strain into a chilled coupe glass

Garnish with a twist of lemon

QUATTRO BIANCHI

ITALY

Quattro Bianchi was huge in the 1990s in clubs. It's essentially a very strong Italian version of a Long Island Iced Tea. The 'four whites' in the cocktail's name are tequila, vodka, gin and white rum – so please handle with care, it's a strong cocktail that's dangerously drinkable!

15ml (½oz) tequila

15ml (½oz) vodka

15ml (½oz) gin

15ml (½oz) white rum

30ml (1oz) freshly squeezed lemon juice

15ml (½oz) simple syrup (see page 12)

Ice: Cubed

Garnish: Lemon wedge

Equipment: Cocktail shaker, strainer

Fill a cocktail shaker with ice

Add all the ingredients

Shake vigorously to combine and chill

Strain into a collins glass filled with ice

Garnish with a wedge of lemon

For a fruity variation, muddle a handful of fresh strawberries (or the fruit of your choice) at the start or replace 15ml (½oz) simple syrup with 22.5ml (¾oz) of your favourite fruit syrup.

FRENCH ROSE

FRANCE

The origins of this simple yet sublime three-ingredient cocktail are said to lie with barman Johnny Mitta of the Hôtel Chatham in Paris in the early 20th century. Any cocktail that showcases Lillet Blanc gets my vote. For years, aromatized wine has bafflingly been left with its nose pressed against the window of the world's best bars and it's great to be reminded of just how uniquely fruity, fragrant and intriguing it can be. Pine, candied orange, scented honey and exotic fruit: what a brilliant and valued cocktail pepper-upper Lillet Blanc is. If I could buy it a drink, I would. And that drink would be a French Rose. Here's to a drink for a drink.

45ml (1½oz) gin

15ml (½oz) cherry brandy

15ml (½oz) Lillet Blanc

Ice: Cubed

Garnish: Maraschino cherry

Equipment: Cocktail shaker, strainer

Fill a cocktail shaker with ice

Add all the ingredients

Shake vigorously to combine and chill

Strain into a chilled cocktail or coupe glass

Garnish with a speared cherry

HUGO

GERMANY (VIA ITALY)

The Hugo (pronounced 'oo-go') was, it is said, invented in 2005 by bartender Roland Gruber in the Italian town of Naturno. It spread across international borders and today is one of the most popular summer cocktails in Germany. Try replacing the mint with lemon balm if you want to mix it up, but whichever herb you choose, Hugo is one heck of a fantastic summery aperitif.

120ml (4oz) prosecco

15ml (½oz) St-Germain elderflower liqueur

30ml (1oz) soda water to top

2 mint sprigs

Ice: Cubed

Garnish: Mint sprig

Equipment: Muddler, long bar spoon

Muddle the mint in the bottom of a wine glass and fill with ice

Add all the ingredients

Stir gently to combine

Garnish with another sprig of mint

CROCKTAIL

CROATIA

This prize-winning cocktail was created by Marin Nekić using local ingredients to help boost tourism and create Croatia's first 'national drink'. It should be raised both to the great Croatian cherry, but also the cravat, a Croatian invention and symbol of elegance. I've never been a fan of wearing ties; however, as I write this I feel my destiny could become eternally entwined with the cravat. World Cravat Day falls on 18th October every year and if you happen to be reading this on that sacred day, tie a cravat loosely and louchely around your neck, assemble these ingredients and give thanks to Marin for the CROcktail.

60ml (2oz) Luxardo maraschino liqueur

30ml (1oz) cherry juice

15ml (½oz) freshly squeezed lime juice

1 slice orange

Ice: Cubed

Garnish: Orange twist

Equipment: Long bar spoon

Muddle a slice of orange in an old fashioned glass and discard the fruit

Fill the glass with ice and add the remaining ingredients

Stir gently to combine and chill

Garnish with a twist of orange

PERROQUET

BETON

FRANCE

CZECHIA/CZECH REPUBLIC

Aaah, the parrot. This cocktail was introduced to me by my mum after several trips to France with her friends. She'd always return with an impressive number of photos of her brandishing a Perroquet in the sunlight, positively beaming in every single shot. And when you taste your first Perroquet, it's easy to understand why. Release your inner parrot and let your plumage shine, just like my dear mum and her merriest twinkle.

This take on the G&T is considered the Czech Republic's national drink. Becherovka, a herbal liqueur, tastes like an echo of the happiest Christmas, with festive notes of cloves, anise, cinnamon, citrus and ginger. Sold as 'English Bitter', it was originally created by Czech pharmacist Josef Vitus Becher as a remedy for stomach problems. Thankfully, stomach problems are not a prerequisite for enjoying this classic cocktail.

30ml (1oz) pastis

7.5ml (¼oz) green peppermint syrup

Still mineral water to top

Ice: Cubed

60ml (2oz) Becherovka

90ml (3oz) tonic water to top

Ice: Cubed

Garnish: Lime wedge

Fill a collins glass with ice

Add the pastis and peppermint syrup

Top up with still mineral water to taste

Fill a collins glass with ice

Add the Becherovka

Top with tonic water

Garnish with a wedge of lime

GREEK MARTINI

(OLLY'S DISCO VERSION)

GREECE

I love a disco and I adore Greece even more.
The inspiration for this cocktail came on one
of my many visits to the special island of
Alonissos, where many of my dreams have
emerged blinking into the bright realm of
actual real life. In many ways I am profoundly
British and yet whenever I go to Greece I feel
a massive connection to the elemental forces
of the land, the sea, history, people, food and
drink. My inner Greek is always on the verge
of an eruption. Ever since I was 19 years old,
I've visited a new part of Greece at least once
every year, except of course during the
pandemic when this recipe for my Greek
Martini was rehearsed, perfected and finally
judged fit to stand as an emblem for my deep
passion for all things Greek. Yamas, my friends,
and may you too find a special place that rises
eternally in your heart.

22.5ml (¾oz) ouzo

22.5ml (¾oz) vanilla vodka

30ml (1oz) freshly squeezed orange juice

30ml (1oz) cherry juice

7.5ml (¼oz) freshly squeezed lime juice

Ice: Cubed

Garnish: Dehydrated orange slice

Equipment: Cocktail shaker, strainer

Fill a cocktail shaker with ice

Add all the ingredients

Strain into a chilled cocktail or coupe glass

Garnish with a dehydrated slice of orange

NUTTY RUSSIAN

RUSSIA

This nutty riff on a Black Russian is a sweet spot for after dinner.

45ml (1½oz) vodka

22.5ml (¾oz) Frangelico hazelnut liqueur

22.5ml (¾oz) Kahlúa coffee liqueur

Ice: Cubed

Equipment: Mixing glass, long bar spoon, strainer

Fill a mixing glass with ice

Add all the ingredients

Stir gently to combine and chill

Strain into an old fashioned glass filled with ice

Splash a little cola on top if you feel like lengthening it a tad. Gorgeous!

MOMISETTE

FRANCE

With its cloudy appearance when diluted with water, pastis earned the nickname 'Petit Jaune' or 'Little Yellow' and was created in the early 20th century after a ban on absinthe. I adore its aromatic anise character, and this cocktail is one you can customize with as much or as little sparkling water as you choose. Keep tasting until you find the balance that works best for you. And then make another for me, please!

30ml (1oz) pastis

7.5ml (¼oz) orgeat syrup

Sparkling water to top

Ice: Cubed

Fill a collins glass with ice

Add the pastis and orgeat

Top up with sparkling water to taste

IRISH MAID

IRELAND

If you're into Whiskey Sours or even Mint Juleps, this scented whiskey cocktail is definitely worth taking out for a spin. Thanks to its floral refreshment it's on the fresher side, so it's also one to shake for those new to whiskey or who aren't regular whiskey drinkers. It's ideal for the warmer months in the great outdoors to refresh and rejoice in.

60ml (2oz) Irish whiskey

15ml (½oz) St-Germain elderflower liqueur

22.5ml (¾oz) freshly squeezed lemon juice

15ml (½oz) honey syrup (see page 14)

2 slices of cucumber

Ice: Cubed

Garnish: Cucumber strip

Equipment: Cocktail shaker, strainer, muddler

Muddle the cucumber in the bottom of a cocktail shaker

Fill with ice and add the remaining ingredients

Shake vigorously to combine and chill

Strain into an old fashioned glass filled with ice

Garnish with a strip of cucumber

THE KINGPIN

UNITED KINGDOM

Rheon Johnson created this brilliant cocktail recipe for The Dandy Bar, a favourite London cocktail haunt of mine at the Mayfair Townhouse on Half Moon Street. It's simply a magical place to be – I love staying in the hotel and whenever I get the chance, I pay The Dandy Bar a visit. Resonating with sweet nutty depth, warming cognac and the genius of the smoked maple syrup (available online), this is a fantastic afternoon sipper to make the world feel like it's woven from dreams. And if you do visit the bar, as well as sipping your Kingpin, you simply have to order a Randy Dandy. It's an invention by Randy Gyedu behind the bar, and I was the first to taste this outstanding blend of Chartreuse, maple syrup, rye whiskey and bitters. In fact, just tell the team the flavours you like most of all and ask them to create you a signature cocktail. Before you know it, you'll be tasting your very own name.

50ml (1¾oz) Rémy Martin 1738

10ml (⅓oz) Frangelico hazelnut liqueur

5ml (⅙oz) smoke-infused maple syrup

3 dashes walnut bitters

Ice: Cubed and large cubed

Garnish: Chocolate stick

Equipment: Mixing glass, long bar spoon, strainer

Fill a mixing glass with ice

Add all the ingredients

Stir gently to combine and chill

Strain into an old fashioned glass with a single large ice block

Garnish with a stick of chocolate

AGUA DE VALENCIA

SPAIN

This 'water of Valencia' was, so the tale goes, introduced in 1959 by Constante Gil who worked in Valencia at the Café Madrid. If you're a fan of Bucks Fizz or Mimosas this is a natural step along the same path and delicious served with nibbles. A celebration of the Valencia orange crop, it's a great one to make for brunch or parties in large batches. Quench and cheer for this joyful bubbly combo.

120ml (4oz) cava to top

30ml (1oz) gin

30ml (1oz) Grand Marnier orange liqueur

90ml (3oz) freshly squeezed Valencia or blood orange juice (or a combination of both)

Ice: Cubed

Garnish: Dehydrated orange slice

Equipment: Long bar spoon

Three-quarters fill a wine glass with cubed ice

Add all the ingredients except the cava

Stir gently to combine and chill

Top with cava and stir gently once more

Garnish with a dehydrated slice of orange

BITTERSWEET PASSION

GREECE

This cocktail was created by Giorgos (George) Bogdanos in one of my favourite cocktail bars in the world: Le Rocher in Loggos, on the Greek island of Paxos. With its rustic setting, the boutique Le Rocher has a terrific team that includes Christos and Spiros Vrachoritis – their hospitality and mellow vibe is immensely soothing and the bar itself has a magical setting right on the water in an ancient building. I particularly love the back terrace by the little beach at sunset (see you there), and the cocktails are all unique, splendid and compelling. This Bittersweet Passion was the favourite of my pal Anna Huckerby on holiday in 2022, so this cocktail is dedicated to her.

I tried very hard but can't resist also mentioning another of Giorgos's recipes that I loved: the **Smoky Gangster** is 20ml (⅔oz) mezcal, 40ml (1⅓oz) tequila blanco, 15ml (½oz) agave syrup, 20ml (⅔oz) lime juice, 2 dashes of lime bitters and 2 dashes of firewater bitters all rolled into a collins glass with ice and topped off with premium ginger ale. Garnish with a sea salt rim – or in a line right down the outside of the glass as they do in the bar – and top with a wheel of burnt lime. Corking!

Yamas to Giorgos and the gang.

50ml (2oz) dry gin

35ml (1¼oz) Aperol

25ml (1oz) passionfruit purée

5ml (⅙oz) Velvet Falernum

10ml (⅓oz) freshly squeezed lime juice

20ml (⅔oz) simple syrup (see page 12)

2 dashes Peychaud's bitters

Ice: Cubed

Garnish: Dehydrated orange slice and mint sprig

Equipment: Cocktail shaker, strainer

Fill a cocktail shaker with ice

Add all the ingredients

Shake vigorously to combine and chill

Strain into a chilled coupe glass

Garnish with a dehydrated slice of orange and a small sprig of mint

BALKAN
BEAUTY

BULGARIA

'A psychotherapist can help you but rakia is cheaper.' So goes the modern-day Bulgarian proverb when rakia (a.k.a. raki) is served to visitors. This clear spirit is most often distilled from plums and grapes but in reality, any fruit will get the job done. There's even a Rakia & Spirits Fest every December in the Bulgarian capital Sofia. In 2022 it promised 'more than 300 kinds of rakia and other spirits to taste from the Balkan region and the world'. Let's go! In the meantime we can revel in this delightful rakia-inspired raspberry-cherry-lime trio of fruity gumption.

30ml (1oz) rakia

15ml (½oz) Luxardo maraschino liqueur

15ml (½oz) raspberry purée

15ml (½oz) freshly squeezed lime juice

2 dashes lemon bitters

Ice: Cubed

Garnish: Raspberries

Equipment: Cocktail shaker, strainer

Fill a cocktail shaker with ice

Add all the ingredients

Shake vigorously to combine and chill

Strain into a rocks glass filled with ice

Garnish with a few fresh raspberries

GIN 707

ITALY

I created this cocktail for the launch of Aston Martin's DBX707, a 4x4 like no other which was being showcased at the Hotel Cala di Volpe in Sardinia. Eagle-eyed James Bond fans will recognize the Cala di Volpe, which features heavily in *The Spy Who Loved Me* during Sir Roger Moore's tenure as 007. As a fan and friend of Roger's, while I shook up this cocktail on the roof terrace of a glamorous private suite, I couldn't help murmuring 'nobody does it better' in homage to His Rogesty. The cocktail has since become a staple in my home and always makes me think of beautifully presented Aston Martins parked on the beach, glimmering in golden sunsets and revelling in the splendour of Sardinia's Costa Smeralda.

60ml (2oz) Cornerstone Rare Cornish Gin

15ml (½oz) Cointreau orange liqueur

30ml (1oz) freshly squeezed lemon juice

15ml (½oz) simple syrup (see page 12)

Pinch dried chilli flakes

Ice: Cubed

Garnish: Orange zest

Equipment: Cocktail shaker, strainer

Fill a cocktail shaker with ice

Add all the ingredients

Shake vigorously to combine and chill

Strain and strain into a chilled cocktail or coupe glass

Garnish with a twist of orange

LUCK OF
THE IRISH

IRELAND

Along with luck, the Emerald Isle is also associated with all things green. Chartreuse may hail from France, but with a completely natural green colour, it fits the bill to add to the intrigue of this recipe. I reckon the taste of green Chartreuse is one of the most complex and fascinating of any liqueurs and I'd almost want to dial down the sweetness a jot to have even greater access to the herbal riddle that lurks within. In this bittersweet cocktail the sweet vermouth, boosted by Irish whiskey, ensures a herbaceous, full-flavoured cocktail with instant aromatic appeal.

30ml (1oz) Irish whiskey

30ml (1oz) sweet vermouth

15ml (½oz) green Chartreuse

2-3 drops mint bitters

Ice: Cubed and large cubed

Garnish: Mint sprig

Equipment: Mixing glass, long bar spoon, strainer

Fill a mixing glass with ice

Add all the ingredients

Stir gently to combine and chill

Strain into an old fashioned glass filled with a large ice cube

Garnish with a small sprig of mint

WHITE NEGRONI

ITALY

For fans of a classic Negroni, this is a great, fun way to mix things up. Created by British bartender Wayne Collins in 2001, The White Negroni riffs on the gin part of a classic Negroni and builds on white vermouth with gentian liqueur. Gentian root comes from the mountains of Europe and it's a fantastic bitter aperitif (try Suze over ice with a squeeze of fresh lemon). For some reason it always makes me think of the mournful resonant saxophone playing 'Betty & Zorg' which opens the soundtrack to the tragic French movie *Betty Blue*. Haunting flavours, moody sounds. In any case, the White Negroni, with its roots in the Italian classic, is a veritable weave of international appeal.

22.5ml (¾oz) gin

22.5ml (¾oz) Suze or other gentian liqueur

22.5ml (¾oz) white vermouth (Lillet Blanc, for example)

2 dashes orange bitters

Ice: Cubed

Garnish: Orange twist

Equipment: Long bar spoon

Fill an old fashioned glass with ice

Add all the ingredients

Stir gently to combine and chill

Garnish with a twist of orange

AMERICANO

ITALY

Softening the bittersweet eruptions of Campari and red vermouth, soda lengthens and grants easier access to the complexities of both. You can experiment with the mixer and use lemonade, ginger beer, orangeade, bitter lemon, tonic water, whatever takes your fancy to customize – and get creative with the garnish too, pink grapefruit is fab! I always find an Americano is the right drink to mix late in the evening to revive flagging spirits: it's so simple to mix in the glass and always instantly delicious.

45ml (1½oz) Campari

45ml (1½oz) sweet red vermouth

Soda water to top

Ice: Cubed

Garnish: Orange slice

Equipment: Long bar spoon

Fill a highball glass with ice

Add all the ingredients

Top with soda water

Stir gently to combine and chill

Garnish with a slice of orange

GREEK SIDECAR

GREECE

Metaxa was created in 1888 by Spyros Metaxas, a silk merchant. Legend has it he wanted his spirit to deliver a similar smoothness. In this take on the Sidecar, it feels like those worlds do indeed collide, with silk and spirit united as one.

45ml (1½oz) Metaxa

22.5ml (¾oz) Cointreau orange liqueur

22.5ml (¾oz) freshly squeezed lemon juice

Ice: Cubed

Garnish: Sugar rim and lemon twist

Equipment: Cocktail shaker, strainer

Fill a cocktail shaker with ice

Add all the ingredients

Shake vigorously to combine and chill

Sugar rim a chilled coupe glass (follow the method for salt rim; see page 11)

Strain into the coupe glass

Garnish with a twist of lemon

FORAGER'S FIZZ

Where I live in Sussex, not far from the county town of Lewes, blackthorn is on the rampage. Since my children were born, we've foraged sloes from these hedgerow bushes for our own range of homemade elixirs, sloe gin in particular. I also used to make the kids a non-alcoholic 'Sloe-bena' by warming the berries with a little water and sugar for a seasonal cordial – it's sensationally fruity and has the most purple-soaked colour you can possibly imagine. This Forager's Fizz came about after experimenting with honey from our own bees and celebrates all that grows wild in abundance in my little corner of the world, elderflower included. I've even got a valiant lemon tree that tries its best to pretend that Sussex is Spain. It is, like me, an eternal optimist.

45ml (1½oz) sloe gin

22.5ml (¾oz) St-Germain elderflower liqueur

15ml (½oz) freshly squeezed lemon juice

7.5ml (¼oz) honey syrup (see page 14)

English sparkling wine to top

Ice: Cubed

Garnish: Lemon twist and edible flowers

Equipment: Cocktail shaker, strainer

Fill a cocktail shaker with ice

Add all the ingredients except the sparkling wine

Shake vigorously to combine and chill

Strain into a collins glass filled with ice

Top with English sparkling wine and stir once to combine

Garnish with a twist of lemon and edible flowers

CREME EI

(OLLY'S CREAM EGG)

GERMANY

This is as close as I have ever come to laying an egg. I love Christmas, but I also adore Easter. The feast, the time of the year, rising birdsong, gentler days and the promise of blooming buds. The Easter bunny began life as the Germanic and Saxon goddess of the dawn and the spring, Ēostre, whose sacred animal was supposedly a hare. In Germany, the Easter hare was said to bring good children a basket of painted eggs, which would be hidden for the children to find. Queen Victoria, whose mother was German, organized egg hunts for her children at Kensington Palace and this helped bring the tradition to Britain. You really couldn't make this stuff up... Oh, hang on, they did! Finally, the tradition of making things up reaches its apotheosis in this cocktail which tastes like a cream egg hatched from the very spirit of a nest of good vibes.

15ml (½oz) rum, brandy or bourbon

15ml (½oz) white crème de cacao

15ml (½oz) advocaat

15ml (½oz) vanilla vodka

2 scoops vanilla ice cream

Ice: Crushed

Garnish: Chocolate shavings

Equipment: Blender

Add all the ingredients to a blender cup with half a scoop of crushed ice

Blend on high to chill and combine

Pour into a chilled wine glass

Garnish with a light sprinkle of shaved dark chocolate (or half an 'Easter cream/sugar-based chocolate egg')

ALBANIA

ALBANIA

Cornelian cherries are particularly famed for their flavour and come from the Albanian Alps, which also go by the rather terrifying name 'the Accursed Mountains'. Their juice is superbly tart and sour. For this recipe, you could easily switch for cranberry juice or a cranberry–cherry juice blend to moderate. Across Albania, raki is considered a bit of a national drink and can be distilled from pretty much any fruit. Pick one with roughly 40% ABV for this cocktail and you're all set for splendour.

37.5ml (1¼oz) raki

60ml (2oz) cornelian cherry juice

7.5ml (¼oz) Underberg bitters

Ice: Cubed

Equipment: Mixing glass, long bar
      spoon, strainer

Fill a mixing glass with ice

Add all the ingredients

Stir gently to combine and chill

Strain into an old fashioned glass
filled with ice

KIRSCH COSMO

GERMANY

The Kirsch Cosmo was invented by Hannah Lanfear of Boisdale in London in 2013. Kirsch is short for Kirschwasser, which literally translates as 'cherry water', but rest assured, this double-distilled fruit spirit, unlike water, has a welcome and reassuring kick to it. As well as tasting like a fruity bonanza, the alluring pink of this tangy cocktail makes it look magnificent.

30ml (1oz) kirsch

30ml (1oz) Cointreau orange liqueur

45ml (1½oz) cranberry juice

15ml (½oz) freshly squeezed lime juice

Ice: Cubed

Garnish: Orange twist

Equipment: Cocktail shaker, strainer

Fill a cocktail shaker with ice

Add all the ingredients

Shake vigorously to combine and chill

Strain into a chilled cocktail or coupe glass

Garnish with a twist of orange

SIBELIUS BLACK PUNCH

FINLAND

Russia may be well known for vodka but Finland runs a close second in terms of famous brands (Finlandia, for instance) and a deep national passion for the drink. Jean Sibelius was a Finnish composer born in 1865 who wrote 'Finlandia', which operates as an unofficial national anthem. Growing up, I was a keen French horn player (grade 8 with distinction, since you ask) and very much enjoyed playing this rather splendid piece as a teenager. I seem to have not played the French horn for a ludicrous amount of time since then, so here's to Sibelius, music and the case of the missing horn.

180ml (6oz) red wine

45ml (1½oz) vodka

30ml (1oz) strong brewed Earl Grey tea, cooled

15ml (½oz) blackberry purée

15ml (½oz) freshly squeezed lime juice

Ice: Cubed

Garnish: Dehydrated orange slice

Equipment: Cocktail shaker, strainer

Fill a cocktail shaker with ice

Add all the ingredients

Shake vigorously to combine and chill

Strain into a collins glass filled with ice

Garnish with a dehydrated slice of orange

FROZEN APEROL SPRITZ

ITALY

A deep-chilled take on the iconic Italian drink sipped in the early evening 'Apero' hour. Aperol was launched in 1919 by Luigi and Silvio Barbieri in Padua, Italy. The low-ish alcohol content allows Italians to sip for a while, watching the world go by – Gucci shades are optional.

45ml (1½oz) Aperol

15ml (½oz) orange vodka

15ml (½oz) freshly squeezed orange juice

15ml (½oz) freshly squeezed lemon juice

15ml (½oz) simple syrup (see page 12)

Dash of grenadine or grenadine syrup (see page 12)

Ice: Crushed

Garnish: Dehydrated orange slice

Equipment: Blender

Add all the ingredients to a blender cup with 1 scoop of crushed ice

Blend on high until you have a smooth, thick cocktail

Tap out into a wine glass

Garnish with a dehydrated slice of orange

NORTHERN LIGHTS DAIQUIRI

NORWAY

You'd be amazed where you can pick up lingonberry syrup these days – a quick search on the internet and you'll have it in no time. And it's well worth getting some for this Nordic take on a Caribbean classic. The Aurora Borealis is somehow like a tropical surge across the deep dark wintry skies of Norway, and it definitely brings colour and lightness whenever you drink it. Skål!

60ml (2oz) Norwegian aquavit

30ml (1oz) freshly squeezed lime juice

15ml (½oz) lingonberry syrup

Ice: Cubed

Garnish: Lime twist

Equipment: Cocktail shaker, strainer

Fill a cocktail shaker with ice

Add all the ingredients

Shake vigorously to combine and chill

Strain into a chilled cocktail or coupe glass

Garnish with a twist of lime

BISON GRASS MARTINI

POLAND

Na zdrowie! Cheers to this celebration of vodka made from bison grass, a centuries-old tradition and the favoured food of bison which still roam the Białowieża forest and beyond. Bright as an apple with a neutron star tucked in its core, this Martini is marvellous to kick off a celebratory gathering - lunch, or indeed a wedding banquet, which in Poland is legendary for dancing as well as the constellations of vodka shots which orbit through several days!

45ml (1½oz) Żubrówka bison grass vodka

15ml (½oz) dry vermouth

15ml (½oz) clear dry apple juice

7.5ml (¼oz) honey syrup (see page 14)

Ice: Cubed

Garnish: Apple slice

Equipment: Cocktail shaker, strainer

Fill a cocktail shaker with ice

Add all the ingredients

Shake vigorously to combine and chill

Strain into a chilled cocktail or coupe glass

Garnish with a thin slice of apple

REBUJITO

The Rebujito is a firm favourite of mine, introduced to me by my friends at the González Byass bodega using Tio Pepe Fino sherry at the Easter Feria celebrations. It's a great one to drink in the heat thanks to its soaring refreshment, a great one also to keep the party going for its scrumptiously easy drinking. If you've ever dismissed sherry, give the Rebujito a whirl for simplicity and surprisingly wide appeal. Great to make in large jugs and batches for parties, barbecues and picnics. Light, bright and sparkling, this cocktail is liquid diamonds.

60ml (2oz) fino sherry

120ml (4oz) lemon-lime soda

10 mint leaves

Ice: Crushed

Garnish: Lemon and lime slices

Equipment: Muddler, long bar spoon

Muddle the mint in the bottom of a collins glass

Three-quarters fill with crushed ice and add the sherry

Top with lemon-lime soda

Stir once to combine and cap with a little more crushed ice

Garnish with a slice of lemon and lime

JÄGERTEE

AUSTRIA

With its very own EU Protected Designation of Origin reserved for Austria, this Jägertee – 'Hunters Tea' – has plenty of welly! Or perhaps that should be boot, since it's so popular on the ski slopes. If you find it too powerful, you can tame the boozy roar by adding 240ml (8oz) of orange juice to the recipe. Stroh spiced rum ('The Spirit of Austria') has been around since 1832, and Stroh Inländer 40, with its cinnamon-treacle richness, is my go-to choice for this cocktail. That said, the double-boozy Inländer 80 is the one to choose for that full 'Have I just swallowed a radiator?' effect.

240ml (8oz) Stroh Austrian rum

240ml (8oz) red wine

240ml (8oz) plum brandy or schnapps

240ml (8oz) black tea, brewed and cooled

2–3 cloves

30g (1oz) brown sugar

4 slices lemon

Equipment: Saucepan

Add all the ingredients to a large, non-reactive saucepan

Heat gently to just below boiling point (do not boil) and simmer for 15–20 minutes

Serve warm in glass mugs

TINTO DE VERANO

Before we were married and when my wife Sophie lived in Seville, Spain, as a student in the late 1990s, we'd gaze up at Hale-Bopp together, a comet that was thundering across the skies in apparent suspended animation for what seemed like months. In the dusty golden Easter warmth suffusing this ancient city's squares and shaded nooks, Tinto de Verano became our drink of choice for daytime delights. It's essentially instant Sangria - and you can change lemon soda for a citrus soda of your choice to mix up flavours. And it's a stunner for barbecues, picnics or just lazy days in the sun. Comets are optional.

750ml (25oz) red wine

120ml (4oz) Spanish red vermouth

750ml (25oz) lemon soda

½ orange, sliced

½ lemon, sliced

Ice: Cubed

Garnish: Lemon and orange slices

Equipment: Long bar spoon

Add the citrus fruits to a pitcher and half-fill with ice

Add all the remaining ingredients and stir

Top with ice and stir once to combine and chill

Serve in chilled glasses

BELLINI

(PUCCINI, ROSSINI AND TINTORETTO)

ITALY

The Bellini cocktail was invented in 1948 by Giuseppe Cipriani, founder of legendary Harry's Bar in Venice. Just off the Grand Canal, this iconic bar has been frequented by the likes of Humphrey Bogart, Truman Capote and Ernest Hemingway. Until your next visit, this blend of white peach and Prosecco will take you there, sip by sip.

120ml (4oz) prosecco

60ml (2oz) white peach purée

Garnish: Peach slice

Equipment: Long bar spoon

Pour the white peach purée into a chilled champagne flute

Tilt the glass and top up with the prosecco

Stir once to combine

Garnish with a thin slice of peach

This sunset-hued cocktail was named after Venetian painter Giovanni Bellini, known for the sumptuous colours of his work. You could always consider variations on the Bellini theme, which reference other Italian notables: to make a **Puccini**, replace the peach with mandarin juice. For a **Rossini**, replace it with strawberry, and to create a **Tintoretto** replace with pomegranate juice. Just make sure you always garnish the glass with the same base fruit of the cocktail.

BLUE LAGOON

NETHERLANDS/CURAÇAO

Okay, this is technically not a cocktail from the Netherlands, but the Caribbean island of Curaçao is a constituent country of the Netherlands! Does that count? Of course! The Lahara orange evolved from oranges planted on the island by the Spanish before the arrival of the Dutch. The trees that flourished in Spain struggled in the arid Caribbean and produced fruit that was fibrous and bitter. However, the peels provided an aromatic oil for the liqueur that became blue curaçao. The blue dye part is a bit of a mystery but since it makes cocktails faintly ludicrous and wildly exotic it gets my vote every time.

30ml (1oz) vodka

30ml (1oz) blue curaçao

15ml (½oz) freshly squeezed lime juice

4oz (4oz) lemonade to top

Ice: Cubed and crushed

Garnish: Cocktail cherry and dehydrated lime wheel

Equipment: Cocktail shaker, strainer, long bar spoon

Fill a cocktail shaker with ice

Add all the ingredients except the lemonade

Shake vigorously to combine and chill

Strain into a hurricane glass filled with crushed ice

Top with lemonade and stir once to combine

Garnish with a cocktail cherry and a dehydrated lime wheel

LONKERO

(A.K.A. THE FINNISH LONG DRINK)

FINLAND

Gin and grapefruit rule the roost in the Lonkero. In Finland you can find the ready-to-drink version everywhere under the Hartwall brand. It was invented in 1952 for the Summer Olympics in Helsinki; Lonkero translates directly as 'tentacle' and also refers generally to long drinks in Finland. I toured the country as a chorister with King's College Cambridge in the 1980s, but alas was a touch too young to latch on to any passing Finnish tentacles. These days, however, this cocktail invariably inspires me to sing, mainly Take That's 'Greatest Day', because, with a cocktail in your hand, it always is.

60ml (2oz) gin

15ml (½oz) cranberry juice

15ml (½oz) freshly squeezed lemon juice

120ml (4oz) grapefruit soda to top

Ice: Cubed and large cubed

Garnish: Pink grapefruit slice

Equipment: Cocktail shaker, strainer

Fill a cocktail shaker with ice

Add all the ingredients except the grapefruit soda

Shake vigorously to combine and chill

Strain into a collins glass filled with ice and top with grapefruit soda

Garnish with a slice of pink grapefruit

FULL MONTE

ITALY

This Full Monte recipe takes a Reverse Manhattan (see page 243) and replaces the vermouth with amaro. With the bittersweet piquancy of Amaro Montenegro, I love a Full Monte after dinner to set the scene for a bit of reflective chinwaggery. Amaro Montenegro was invented in 1885 by Stanislao Cobianchi using 40 different herbs, fruits and botanicals. He called it *Elisir Lungavita* (elixir of long life), but renamed it after Princess Elena of Montenegro who married the future king of Italy... so you never quite know where a Full Monte might lead.

60ml (1oz) Amaro Montenegro

30ml (2oz) rye whiskey

Dash of Angostura bitters

Dash of orange bitters

Ice: Cubed and large cubed

Garnish: Orange twist

Equipment: Mixing glass, long bar spoon, strainer

Fill a mixing glass with ice

Add all the ingredients

Stir gently to combine and chill

Strain into an old fashioned glass filled with a large ice cube

Garnish with a twist of orange

HUNTER'S TEA

Similar to Austrian Jägertee (see page 145), this German version uses the famous, and seemingly ubiquitous, Jägermeister, a digestif with 56 herbs and spices, made to a secret, closely guarded recipe and inspired by hunters (the deer on the bottle is a nod to this). It is entirely vegan; however, thanks in part to the deer on the label, some people erroneously believe it was once made with deer's blood. The company insists this has never been the case – all I'll say is that it tastes far better than you remember and contributes magnificently to this cuppa of a cocktail.

45ml (1½oz) Jägermeister

45ml (1½oz) black tea, brewed and cooled

15ml (½oz) freshly squeezed lime juice

7.5ml (¼oz) maple syrup

Ice: Cubed

Garnish: Lemon twist

Equipment: Cocktail shaker, strainer

Fill a cocktail shaker with ice

Add all the ingredients

Shake vigorously to combine and chill

Strain into an old fashioned glass filled with ice

Garnish with a twist of lemon

GREEK
TRAGEDY

An equal-parter of a drink, this Greek Tragedy is anything but sad, although it certainly feels cathartic. Deep thoughts almost always come to me with every anise-infused sip. Chambord's raspberry revs create a powerful vortex which entices sweet vermouth's red-fruit depth into the spinning centre and from the apex bursts anise via ouzo like a reverse black hole... and serenity is restored.

22.5ml (¾oz) ouzo

22.5ml (¾oz) Chambord raspberry liqueur

22.5ml (¾oz) sweet vermouth

15ml (½oz) freshly squeezed lime juice

Ice: Cubed

Garnish: Lime twist and cocktail cherry

Equipment: Cocktail shaker, strainer

Fill a cocktail shaker with ice

Add all the ingredients

Shake vigorously to combine and chill

Strain into a chilled coupe glass

Garnish with a twist of lime and a speared cherry

FROZEN SZARLOTKA

POLAND

Pronounced 'shar-lot-ka', Szarlotka is Poland's prized traditional apple cake. The largest apple-growing country in northern Europe, Poland has been in the orchard game for centuries and this cocktail tastes like the best apple pie your mind can conjure. With the gold flakes in your bottle of Goldschläger schnapps you could squint a bit and imagine them to be the falling leaves of burnished autumn beauty in the orchard, or just blend it into this drink for its sweet cinnamon caress.

45ml (1½oz) Żubrówka bison grass vodka

7.5ml (¼oz) Goldschläger cinnamon schnapps

90ml (3oz) cloudy apple juice

1 tsp vanilla paste

Ice: Crushed

Garnish: Cinnamon stick and apple slice

Equipment: Blender

Add all the ingredients to a blender cup with 1 scoop of crushed ice

Blend on high until you have a smooth, thick cocktail

Tap out into a wine glass

Garnish with a cinnamon stick and a thin slice of apple

BLACK VELVET

IRELAND

My in-laws live near Ballyferriter on Ireland's Dingle Peninsula. When you travel this far west your soul becomes the weather, and while my wife Sophie is drawn to the sea, the hills are always calling my name. Memories abound of climbing Mount Brandon followed by a few pints of the black stuff in the village then a trail into Dingle for adventures in two of the world's greatest pubs, Foxy John's and Dick Mack's (who also make terrific beer). The Black Velvet may have an international and slightly sombre heart: it was supposedly created in London to mark the passing of Prince Albert in 1861, but for me, it's a celebratory drink that always makes me think of my love for the music and magic of Dingle. Whether I'm having dinner at Rules in London (which serves an excellent Black Velvet) or at home raising a glass to St Patrick's Day, the Black Velvet is a thing of splendour to kick off a session. Or punctuate one. Or finish one off.

75ml (2½oz) champagne

75ml (2½oz) Guinness

Gently pour both ingredients into a chilled champagne flute

BLOOD
AND
SAND

UNITED KINGDOM

This cocktail is named after the bullfighter film *Blood and Sand* starring Rudolph Valentino, with the redness in the cocktail linking it with the film's title. It's a magnificent classic and one of the few that uses Scotch whisky; it famously appears in Harry Craddock's 1930 *Savoy Cocktail Book* – it's a total gem of a tome for all drinks fans.

22.5ml (¾oz) Scotch whisky

22.5ml (¾oz) Heering cherry liqueur

22.5ml (¾oz) sweet red vermouth

22.5ml (¾oz) freshly squeezed blood orange juice

Ice: Cubed

Garnish: Orange twist

Equipment: Cocktail shaker, strainer

Fill a cocktail shaker with ice

Add all the ingredients

Shake vigorously to combine and chill

Strain into a chilled cocktail or coupe glass

Garnish with a twist of orange

ZWACK AND SODA

HUNGARY

I love Unicum: deeply embedded somewhere in its sweet, dark core it has a pulsating ring that reminds me of peppermint. It feels like a vintage herb garden has been pressed between the pages of a book of spells and conjured into an elixir of extraordinariness. It's owned by the Zwack family – who have the best surname in the world – and its circular, potion-like bottle holds more than 40 herbs with a history stretching back to the late 1700s. One sip of this amber cocktail and Unicum's nationally adored status in Hungary becomes all too easy to appreciate. Flaming the citrus peel releases a kink of rich fragrance that hovers like a halo over this sacred cocktail – it's a holy tribute with which to venerate all things Hungarian.

45ml(1½oz) Zwack Unicum

22.5ml (¾oz) freshly squeezed lime juice

7.5ml (¼oz) simple syrup (see page 12)

Soda water to top

Orange and lemon zest, one piece each

Ice: Crushed

Garnish: Mint sprig

Equipment: Lighter, long bar spoon

Carefully warm the orange and lemon zests with a small flame, then with your thumb and forefinger squeeze over the collins glass

Three-quarters fill with crushed ice and add all the ingredients except the soda water

Stir gently to combine and top with soda water

Stir once more and cap with crushed ice

Garnish with a sprig of mint

PONCHA

Aguardente de cana is Madeiran sugar-cane spirit, fiery and fabulous, it's a bit like sipping hot laughter. From the early 1400s, Madeira's role in supplying sugar to Europe was underpinned by the exploitation of African slaves. Production grew until the 1500s when it became the biggest exporter of sugar in the world. Today, the local aguardente is vital to the ubiquitous Poncha of which there are myriad variations. Technically a type of rhum agricole, you're going to love a Poncha if you enjoy the light bright flavours of Caipirinhas, this recipe is a peacock with a citrus fantail, dazzling and unforgettably striking.

60ml (2oz) aguardente de cana

45ml (1½oz) freshly squeezed lemon juice

45ml (1½oz) freshly squeezed orange juice

22.5ml (¾oz) freshly squeezed grapefruit juice

15ml (½oz) honey syrup (see page 14)

Ice: Cubed

Garnish: Orange or blood orange slice

Equipment: Cocktail shaker, strainer

Fill a cocktail shaker with ice

Add all the ingredients

Shake vigorously to combine and chill

Strain into a collins glass filled with ice

Garnish with an orange slice

BECHARITA

CZECHIA/CZECH REPUBLIC

If you love a Margarita you'll adore a Becharita, here resurrected in a recipe by drinks pro Simon Ford, although the origin of the first recipe is somewhat shrouded in mystery. Either way, it tastes great; boasting more than 20 herbs and spices, Becherovka, the Czech national liqueur, has subtle notes of anise, cinnamon and ginger and has been produced from the same secret recipe for more than 200 years. And since you're making this cocktail, why not treat yourself to a chilled neat chaser of Becherovka? It's magic, like hearing Janis Joplin's rootsy roar calling from deep within your mind.

60ml (2oz) reposado tequila

30ml (1oz) Becherovka

60ml (2oz) peach nectar

30ml (1oz) freshly squeezed lime juice

15ml (½oz) simple syrup (see page 12)

Ice: Cubed

Garnish: Peach slice and lime wedge

Equipment: Cocktail shaker, strainer

Fill a cocktail shaker with ice

Add all the ingredients

Shake vigorously to combine and chill

Strain into a highball glass filled with ice

Garnish with a slice of peach and a lime wedge

ALBERTO

A late 1930s aperitif cocktail invented in Britain, the Alberto deserves a revival. It's potent and will appeal to fans of Negronis. My personal ritual is to make an Alberto and listen to Al Bowlly singing like the prince of heartbeats. Al is the original crooner and blessed with one of the most beautiful voices of all time. Somehow the overlapping era of his music and this cocktail unite in moments of fondly melancholic romance and the sweetest contemplation. 'Hang Out the Stars in Indiana' always makes me gently dance and sway, and if you fancy playing 'The Very Thought of You', I'm up for making the next round of Albertos.

30ml (1oz) gin

30ml (1oz) Cocchi Americano

30ml (1oz) fino sherry

7.5ml (¼oz) Cointreau orange liqueur

Ice: Cubed

Garnish: Orange twist

Equipment: Mixing glass, long bar spoon, strainer

Fill a mixing glass with ice

Add all the ingredients

Stir gently to combine and chill

Strain into a chilled coupe glass

Garnish with a twist of orange

JENEVER PEAR COLLINS

BELGIUM

Belgium is a proud pear producer and it's a fruit that deserves more love in cocktails, just like this Collins with its rounded refreshment. Jenever is famed across Belgium (and Holland), and you can still find it produced in rather lovely traditional clay vessels. It comes both oude (old) and jonge (young), which rather than age refers to style. Oude is generally a little sweeter, containing more than 15% malt wine, and generally bristles with more botanicals. Jonge has less than 15% malt wine and tends to be lighter and more refreshing. The choice is yours!

60ml (2oz) jenever

45ml (1½oz) pear purée

22.5ml (¾oz) freshly squeezed lemon juice

7.5ml (¼oz) demerara syrup (see page 13)

Soda water to top

Ice: Cubed

Garnish: Lemon wedge

Equipment: Cocktail shaker, strainer

Fill a cocktail shaker with ice

Add all the ingredients except the soda water

Shake vigorously to combine and chill

Strain into a collins glass filled with ice and top with soda water

Garnish with a wedge of lemon

NORMANDIE 75

The apple's answer to the French 75. The first recorded mention of apple brandy was by the fantastically named Lord de Gouberville, Gilles Picot, in 1553. Distillation was already part of French life and several hundred different varieties of apple are found in orchards across Normandy today. I haven't tasted all of them via that fiery fury calvados yet... but I'd love to give it go.

75ml (2½oz) Normandy dry cider

45ml (1½oz) calvados

15ml (½oz) freshly squeezed lemon juice

7.5ml (¼oz) grenadine or grenadine syrup (see page 12)

7.5ml (½oz) simple syrup (see page 12)

Ice: Cubed

Garnish: Lemon twist

Equipment: Cocktail shaker, strainer

Fill a cocktail shaker with ice

Add all the ingredients except the cider

Shake vigorously to combine and chill

Strain into a chilled flute glass and top with cider

Garnish with a twist of lemon

PINK GIN

UNITED KINGDOM

Not to be confused with pink gins infused with red fruit, this is all about the intensely bitter beauty of Angostura bitters. Here it's lengthened, softened and tamed by gin, but you can still taste the full aromatic spicy spectrum of the bitters. And I love that pink hue – it's a slow sipper for all seasons.

60ml (2oz) gin

3–4 dashes Angostura bitters

Ice: Cubed

Garnish: Lemon twist

Equipment: Mixing glass, long bar spoon, strainer

Fill a mixing glass with ice

Add all the ingredients

Stir gently to combine and chill

Strain into a chilled cocktail or coupe glass

Garnish with a twist of lemon

BLUSHIN' RUSSIAN

RUSSIA

Russia is home to the coldest inhabited village in the world. Winters in Oymyakon average minus 50 degrees Celsius so you can see how 'little water' (a.k.a. vodka) might come in handy to keep your actual soul from freezing over. In small doses, of course. Allied here to a creamy conundrum of sweet almond and coffee this is a great variation for fans of the White Russian to taste and help keep your inner spirit level perfectly balanced.

30ml (1oz) vodka

30ml (1oz) Kahlúa coffee liqueur

30ml (1oz) amaretto

30ml (1oz) single cream

Ice: Cubed

Garnish: Coffee beans

Equipment: Cocktail shaker, strainer

Fill a cocktail shaker with ice

Add all the ingredients

Shake vigorously to combine and chill

Strain into a chilled cocktail or coupe glass

Garnish with 2–3 coffee beans

BOBBY BURNS

This one is a cracker for St Andrew's Day, something a little different for Burns Night, a fun drink to sip alongside haggis or a piece of shortbread for a sweeter pairing. Make this drink in honour of Scotland, a place I called home for many years and where my mum's side of the family come from. If I could drink this cocktail anywhere in the world it would be at the summit of Suilven in Assynt, a peak that I claimed with my family – I'd raise my glass with the words of the sublime Scottish poet Norman MacCaig as he crests the top of Suilven into the light and says: 'My shadow jumps huge miles away from me.'

45ml (1½oz) blended Scotch whisky

45ml (1½oz) sweet red vermouth

15ml (½oz) Bénédictine

Ice: Cubed

Garnish: Lemon twist

Equipment: Mixing glass, long bar spoon, strainer

Fill a mixing glass with ice

Add all the ingredients

Stir gently to combine and chill

Strain into a chilled cocktail or coupe glass

Garnish with a twist of lemon

KVASYA

Kvass (pronounced 'ku-vas') is a bit like an ancient Russian probiotic rye bread drink which you can find these days online. It's low in booze (around 1.5%) and in this recipe, vodka brings the hooch. Mix them together, add cinnamon flavouring, and behold, you've made Kvasya.

45ml (1½oz) kvass

15ml (½oz) vodka

7.5ml (¼oz) cinnamon syrup (see page 12)

Ice: Cubed and large cubed

Equipment: Mixing glass, long bar spoon

Fill a mixing glass with ice

Add all the ingredients

Stir gently to combine and chill

Strain into an old fashioned glass filled with a large ice cube

REKYA POMEGRANATE AND MINT FIZZ

ICELAND

Iceland always reminds me of the purity and beauty of the naked landscape. It feels like there's nowhere to hide from the power of the elements, which have been sculpting their ridges for aeons – and hidden forces beneath your feet are ready to erupt at any moment. Reyka vodka is made with glacial spring water filtered through 4,000-year-old lava stones and is richly textured with immense purity and a discreet, aniseed-like echo. Fuelled by renewable geothermal energy, the distillery behind the world's first 'green' vodka is truly small batch and a bit of an icon for Iceland.

45ml (1½oz) Reyka vodka

45ml (1½oz) pomegranate juice

15ml (½oz) freshly squeezed lime juice

Soda water to top

8 mint leaves

8 pomegranate arils (seeds)

Ice: Crushed

Garnish: Mint sprig and pomegranate seeds

Equipment: Muddler, long bar spoon

Muddle the mint in the bottom of a collins glass and drop in the pomegranate arils

Three-quarters fill with crushed ice and add all the ingredients except the soda water

Churn gently with a bar spoon to combine and top with soda water

Churn once more and cap with crushed ice

Garnish with a sprig of mint and a small handful of pomegranate seeds

FRENCH CONNECTION

FRANCE

This is a true 1970s classic drink based on the film of the same name starring Gene Hackman. Gene won an Oscar for Best Actor at the 44th Academy Awards for his performance in *The French Connection*, which followed his NYPD detective Jimmy 'Popeye' Doyle busting a narcotics ring based in Marseille. This cocktail is long overdue an accolade for its simplicity and scrumptiousness, and reminds me of a trip I once made to Marseille in my teenage years with my dear friend Jim Brown. We innocently found ourselves staying in a hotel of dubious repute, but happily came through the experience entirely unscathed. Except for my white boxer shorts emblazoned with red hearts, which were pinched from my room. Looking back, that's clearly a blessing.

45ml (1½oz) cognac

45ml (1½oz) amaretto

Ice: Cubed

Garnish: Lemon twist

Equipment: Long bar spoon

Fill a rocks glass with ice

Add all the ingredients

Stir gently to combine and chill

Garnish with a twist of lemon

NORDIC SUMMER

DENMARK

Who doesn't love a bit of cultish effigy burning? This cocktail is a tradition on Midsummer's Day in Denmark, where it is sipped around huge beach bonfires with Danish snobrød or twisty bread, which is baked over hot coals. The bonfires are lit in Denmark on Sankt Hans evening when songs are enjoyed with family and friends and a wooden figure (often depicting a witch) is burned. I'm thinking about creating a new sort of festival where we build libraries of cocktails then share them together. Often.

60ml (2oz) Aperol

30ml (1oz) aquavit

30ml (1oz) freshly squeezed lime juice

Ice: Cubed

Garnish: Lime twist and orange twist

Equipment: Cocktail shaker, strainer

Fill a cocktail shaker with ice

Add all the ingredients

Shake vigorously to combine and chill

Strain into a chilled cocktail or coupe glass

Garnish with a twist of lime and a twist of orange

GLÜHWEIN

A warm drink to make you glow – indeed, the name Glühwein is said to originate from the red-hot irons that were used to heat the wine ('glüh' = glow). The Romans were big fans of hot spiced wine and across Europe you still find variations on this theme today: French vin chaud, Nordic glögg, British mulled wine and glühwein across Austria and Germany. Spicing and sweetening wine at Christmas is a simple classic with the added bonus of making the house smell as festive as Father Christmas's secret bubble bath.

750ml (25oz) dry red wine

60ml (2oz) freshly squeezed lemon juice

70g (2.5oz) unrefined golden caster sugar

3 cloves

1 cinnamon stick

300ml (10oz) water

1 orange, cut into bite-size pieces

Equipment: Saucepan

Add all the ingredients to a large, non-reactive saucepan

Heat gently to just below boiling point (do not boil) and simmer for 15-20 minutes

Serve warm in glühwein mugs

1789

FRANCE

The French Revolution began with the storming of the Bastille in 1789 and this French classic is a homage to the republic and the social values of 'liberté, égalité, fraternité', which I gratefully salute to this day. Inequality, misuse of power and division have no place between the covers of the *World Cocktail Atlas*. And let's also pay homage to the origin of the obscure fortified elixir Bonal Gentiane-Quina, which was created by former monk Brother Raphael Bonal in the Chartreuse Mountains in 1865. Today it's made by Maison Dolin and is still a bittersweet beauty, rather like the origins of freedom in the struggle of the French Revolution. Here's to 1789.

45ml (1½oz) cognac

15ml (½oz) Lillet Blanc

15ml (½oz) Bonal Gentiane-Quina

Ice: Cubed

Garnish: Orange twist

Equipment: Cocktail shaker, strainer

Fill a cocktail shaker with ice

Add all the ingredients

Shake vigorously to combine and chill

Strain into a chilled cocktail or coupe glass

Garnish with a twist of lemon

BARA BRITH SOUR

WALES

I love Wales. I spent many happy months in that wonderful country surrounded by the warmth of the locals while filming *The Secret Supper Club* for Channel 4, among other shows. Speckled bread or bara brith is a brilliant Welsh tea loaf, and its flavours are echoed in the local whisky. Penderyn is a distillery I adore; keep an eye out too for Aber Falls, Dà Mhìle and more. There was a time when Welsh whisky was subdued by the temperance movement, but with a long history dating back hundreds of years, it's awesome to see so many Welsh whiskies now. I celebrate their rich, vibrant, fruity core – and raise this cocktail to all my Welsh friends for their kind welcome over the years. Lechyd da!

60ml (2oz) Welsh whisky

30ml (1oz) freshly squeezed lemon juice

15ml (½oz) Bara Brith syrup (see page 15)

2 drops Earl Grey bitters

15ml (½oz) egg white

Ice: Cubed

Equipment: Cocktail shaker, strainer

Add all the ingredients to a cocktail shaker without ice. Dry shake for 30 seconds to combine and break down the egg white

Fill the cocktail shaker with ice and shake again to chill

Strain into an old fashioned glass filled with ice

DUTCH OBLIGED

We owe the roots of gin to Holland via their love for jenever and this citrus-soaring cocktail is for grateful gin and jenever fans the world over. For Sunday mornings or Friday nights, this lip-smacker gets you right back in gear and ready for the rigours of sheer pleasure. The windmills of Holland famously ground the grain used for jenever and the flavours in this drink are driven like citrus sails around one another, the orange triple sec tumbling through the pink grapefruit and the jolt of bright jenever winking at its core.

45ml (1½oz) jenever

22.5ml (¾oz) triple sec

22.5ml (¾oz) freshly squeezed pink grapefruit juice

15ml (½oz) honey syrup (see page 14)

2 dashes grapefruit bitters

Ice: Cubed

Garnish: Cocktail cherry

Equipment: Cocktail shaker, strainer

Fill a cocktail shaker with ice

Add all the ingredients

Shake vigorously to combine and chill

Strain into a chilled coupe glass

Garnish with a speared cherry

BEETROOT MARY

UKRAINE

Borscht, the distinctive red soup made from beetroot, is a big deal in Ukraine and considered a symbol of unity. My heart goes out to the people of this mighty land whose heart, courage and steadfast grit has been humbling and inspiring to the world. I raise this to you, your families and the future. Slava Ukraini. Слава Україні!

45ml (1½oz) Ukrainian vodka

90ml (3oz) beetroot juice

30ml (1oz) V8 vegetable juice (or tomato juice)

15ml (½oz) dill pickle brine

3-4 dashes hot sauce

3-4 dashes Worcestershire sauce

1 tsp creamed horseradish (optional)

Pinch of sea salt and cracked pepper

Ice: Cubed

Garnish: Dill pickle and dill frond

Equipment: Long bar spoon

Fill a collins glass with ice

Add all the ingredients except the juices

Stir to combine

Top with the juices and stir once more

Garnish with a speared pickle and a dill frond

SUMMER
RAKI PUNCH

TURKEY

Raki is the national drink of Turkey made from
twice-distilled grapes and aniseed. Clear
when you first pour, it turns cloudy, like pastis,
when water, ice or soda is added and has
been dubbed 'Lion's Milk' due to its fierce
potency. Etiquette is generally never to drink
Raki alone, always in company, which works
a charm for this cocktail as it's an excellent one
to share with a crowd in summertime. A great
one for that day-off sensation when the coals
start to smoke on the barbecue and brilliant
to sip with impactful flavours such as rubs,
marinades and dressings. Summer Raki
Punch is ready to rock.

45ml (1½oz) raki

15ml (½oz) triple sec

30ml (1oz) pomegranate juice

30g (1oz) watermelon purée

6-8 mint leaves

Lemon-lime soda to top

Ice: Cubed and crushed

Garnish: Small wedge of watermelon and mint sprig

Equipment: Muddler, cocktail shaker, strainer,
    long bar spoon

Muddle the watermelon and mint in the bottom of
a cocktail shaker and fill with ice

Add all the ingredients except the lemon-lime soda

Shake vigorously to combine and chill

Strain into a collins glass filled with crushed ice

Top with lemon-lime soda and churn once with
a bar spoon

Garnish with a wedge of watermelon and a sprig
of mint

THE MONET

FRANCE

I created this with my daughter Ruby on 5th December 2022, the anniversary of the day that Claude Monet's spirit passed through the great leaf-blower into the sky. I've always loved Monet's artistry and his garden at Giverny inspired me from an early age to dig and fossick through the soil to tease out life and build a canopy for small creatures to buzz, feed and find refuge in. A great book that is widely available on the secondhand market for bargain prices is *Monet's Garden: Through the Seasons at Giverny* by Vivian Russell, which I warmly recommend reading while sipping this cocktail. The Monet, named for Claude, has Chartreuse for springtime flowers and herbs, a grating of lime zest as an echo of summer grass clippings, gin to celebrate the autumn berries of juniper, egg white for the fluffy, pale winter season and lemon for the bounty of the annual harvest. It's balanced rather precisely and came to Ruby and me spontaneously – your only obligation, if you would, is to raise your glass to the memory of dear Claude.

50ml (2oz) green Chartreuse (or génépi)

50ml (2oz) gin

25ml (1oz) egg white

25ml (1oz) freshly squeezed lemon juice

Ice: Cubed

Garnish: Grated lime zest

Equipment: Cocktail shaker, strainer

Fill a cocktail shaker with ice

Add all the ingredients

Shake vigorously to combine and chill

Strain into a chilled coupe glass

Garnish with a fine grating of lime zest over the surface of the cocktail

JENEVER SOUR

You could say that gin and jenever are the same but different. Juniper is the headline botanical in both, but while the raw material of gin can be pretty much anything (from malted barley to grapes and potatoes), jenever is a blend of malt wine (think mini-whisky minus barrel) and neutral spirit – and generally tends to have less intense juniper vibes. I find there's more of a mellow sweetness to jenever, which is a must-taste drink if you ever visit Belgium and Holland. On a trip to Amsterdam in 2022 the bartender served my jenever brimful in a tiny tulip-shaped glass and insisted on the tradition of me holding my hands behind my back, leaning over for the first sip and alternating further sips with a frosty-cold beer. Europe, I love you.

60ml (2oz) jenever

30ml (1oz) freshly squeezed lemon juice

30ml (1oz) honey syrup (see page 14)

15ml (½oz) egg white

Ice: Cubed

Garnish: Lemon bitters

Equipment: Cocktail shaker, strainer

Fill a cocktail shaker with ice

Add all the ingredients

Shake vigorously to combine and chill

Strain into a chilled coupe glass

Garnish with three dots of lemon bitters on the foam top, then drag a cocktail stick through the centre of each to make three heart shapes

OUZINI

CYPRUS

The Ouzini was created for a Visit Cyprus campaign and focuses on local ingredients to make a fantastic alternative to the ever-popular Cypriot Brandy Sour (see page 190). This refreshing mix of native Cypriot ingredients was invented by Dr Michael Paraskos who also happens to be a novelist and a lecturer in art history and culture at Imperial College, London. Yamas, to the many talents of Michael!

30ml (1oz) ouzo

90ml (3oz) freshly squeezed orange juice

30ml (1oz) freshly squeezed lemon juice

Ice: Cubed

Garnish: Orange slice, 2 dashes of orange bitters

Equipment: Cocktail shaker, strainer

Fill a cocktail shaker with ice

Add all the ingredients

Shake vigorously to combine and chill

Strain into a highball glass filled with ice

Garnish with a slice of orange and 2 dashes of orange bitters

NIKITA

I first dived into a Nikita on the island of
Madeira. As a kid I always loved ice-cream
floats and ice-cream sodas, so when I
discovered this beauty after a wonderful
day leading a shore excursion to Blandy's
winery for P&O Cruises, it was the most
beautiful - if delightfully bonkers - discovery.
It's apparently named after the 1985 Elton
John song 'Nikita' by a fellow called Marcelino,
who was reputed to have invented the drink
in the fishing village of Câmara de Lobos,
also in 1985. Mixing beer and wine may seem
off key but they find a peculiar harmony in
this blend – and you could even add a splash
of dark rum for a little extra party time.

60ml (2oz) light Portuguese beer

60ml (2oz) vinho verde white wine

120g (4oz) fresh pineapple

2 scoops vanilla ice cream

Ice: Crushed

Garnish: Pineapple wedge and cocktail cherry

Equipment: Blender

Add all the ingredients to a blender cup
with 1 scoop of crushed ice

Blend on high to chill and combine

Pour into a chilled collins glass

Garnish with a wedge of pineapple speared with
a cherry

OLLY'S TURKISH DELIGHT COCKTAIL

TURKEY

I am obsessed with Turkish Delight. It's one of my favourite treats; nothing beats its symphonic scented headiness, wavering between exotic, sensual and profoundly perfumed flavour. I find it subsumes my entire being, uniquely so as I often love a hit of spice as well as cutting sharpness in drinks. But this is way different; it's a precise bullseye in the core of all things mellow, yet has the spectacular intensity of Serena Williams serving a tightly bound knot of flowers right to the back of your face. I love it. Hope you do too!

45ml (1½oz) vanilla vodka

15ml (½oz) rose petal vodka (or rose syrup; see page 12)

15ml (½oz) white crème de cacao

7.5ml (¼oz) honey syrup (see page 14)

7.5ml (¼oz) freshly squeezed lemon juice

Dash of grenadine or grenadine syrup (see page 12)

15ml (½oz) egg white

Ice: Cubed

Garnish: Sugar rim and rose petals

Equipment: Cocktail shaker, strainer

Add all the ingredients to a cocktail shaker and dry shake for 30 seconds to break down the egg white

Fill the cocktail shaker with ice and shake vigorously to chill

Strain into a chilled coupe glass rimmed with sugar (follow the method for salt rim, see page 11)

Garnish with edible rose petals

CYPRIOT BRANDY SOUR

(TRADITIONAL TAVERNA RECIPE)

CYPRUS

Cyprus is home to some of the highest vineyards in Europe. In the Troodos Mountains vines stretch up to 1,400m (4,593 feet) with the diurnal range between day and night temperature preserving zing in the grapes. The zesty local Xynisteri white grape often makes its way into the local brandy – it works a charm alongside Cypriot lemons, since they're considered true bitter lemons with their searing acid and high juice content.

45ml (1½oz) Cyprus brandy

22.5ml (¾oz) Cypriot lemon cordial

2 dashes Angostura bitters

Soda water or lemonade to top

Ice: Cubed

Garnish: Lemon–cherry flag

Equipment: Long bar spoon

Fill a collins glass with ice

Dash in bitters then add the brandy and lemon cordial

Top with soda water (or lemonade if you prefer a sweeter cocktail)

Stir gently to combine and chill

Garnish with a lemon–cherry flag

ȚUICĂ COCKTAIL

ROMANIA

Romania is famous for its castles, monasteries, the beautiful Carpathian Mountains and the Black Sea and of course, Dracula, Vlad the Impaler. Perhaps less well known is the country's national drink, Țuică. This Romanian brandy is crafted from fermented and distilled plums, one of Romania's most bountiful crops. Often concocted in makeshift, charcoal-stoked backyard distilleries, Romanians have been making this moonshine since medieval times.

60ml (2oz) Țuică

30ml (1oz) apricot liqueur

15ml (½oz) freshly squeezed lemon juice

15ml (½oz) tonka bean syrup (see page 14)

2 dashes Creole bitters

Ice: Cubed

Garnish: Lemon twist and cocktail cherry

Equipment: Cocktail shaker, strainer

Fill a cocktail shaker with ice

Add all the ingredients

Shake vigorously to combine and chill

Strain into a chilled cocktail or coupe glass

Garnish with a twist of lemon and a cocktail cherry

AQUASPRESSO MARTINI

NORWAY

Norway loves coffee and coffee loves cocktails! This is a fantastic riff on the Espresso Martini and celebrates Norwegian aquavit, which is a protected name under EU law. Norwegian potatoes, aged for more than six months in oak barrels and flavoured with dill or caraway seeds, are all part of the deal in this unique liquid Nordic magic, and all their subtle complexity weaves seamlessly into this party-starter of a drink!

45ml (1½oz) Norwegian aquavit (try the traditional Atlungstad Aquavit No. 1 or seek out bottles made by Egge Gård)

15ml (½oz) vanilla vodka

15ml (½oz) Kahlúa coffee liqueur

7.5ml (¼oz) demerara syrup (see page 13)

30ml (1oz) freshly brewed espresso coffee, cooled

Ice: Cubed

Garnish: Coffee beans

Equipment: Cocktail shaker, strainer

Fill a cocktail shaker with ice

Add all the ingredients

Shake vigorously to combine and chill

Strain into a chilled cocktail or coupe glass

Garnish with 3 coffee beans

MILANO TORINO

The famous Mi-To is a Friday night classic at Smith Towers. Seconds to make, ages to enjoy. It was created in the 1860s and considered the precursor to the Negroni and the Americano, named for the birthplace of Campari (Milano) and Vermouth which traditionally came from Torino a.k.a. Turin. This is one the most portable cocktails in the world: if you're camping and only have egg cups to hand you can always measure out equal quantities of the two red romps and mix them with giant chunks of ice and a slab of orange. Bliss.

45ml (1½oz) Campari

45ml (1½oz) sweet red vermouth

Ice: Cubed and large cubed

Garnish: Dehydrated orange slice

Equipment: Long bar spoon

Fill an old fashioned glass with ice

Add all the ingredients

Stir gently to combine and chill

Garnish with a dehydrated slice of orange

North America

JAMAICAN
TIKI TWIST

JAMAICA

This tiki-style fruity cocktail served in a hurricane glass typifies the kind of drink you'd expect to see by the beach on holiday in the Caribbean. Here's to an epic carnival of tropical flair.

60ml (2oz) white Jamaica rum

30ml (1oz) coconut rum

60ml (2oz) freshly squeezed orange juice

60ml (2oz) cranberry juice

30ml (1oz) passionfruit nectar

22.5ml (¾oz) freshly squeezed lime juice

15ml (½oz) grenadine or grenadine syrup (see page 12)

Ice: Cubed

Garnish: Passionfruit half and a mint sprig

Equipment: Cocktail shaker, strainer

Fill a cocktail shaker with ice

Add all the ingredients

Shake vigorously to combine and chill

Strain into a hurricane glass filled with ice

Garnish with half a passionfruit and a sprig of mint

BARBARY COAST

UNITED STATES OF AMERICA

You can make this drink longer by pouring it straight from the shaker into a tall glass (no need to strain) and topping with soda. As it is though, it's a beauty. Its origins are a little sketchy: it was perhaps created during Prohibition to mask the taste of shonky spirits, or was possibly named after a late-19th and early-20th century red-light district frequented by sailors in San Francisco. All I know is that it's less sweet than you might imagine, with a punchy gloss that washes you up on altogether fairer shores than those roguish sailors.

22.5ml (¾oz) blended Scotch whisky

22.5ml (¾oz) gin

22.5ml (¾oz) white crème de cacao

22.5ml (¾oz) single cream

Ice: Cubed

Garnish: Grated nutmeg

Equipment: Cocktail shaker, strainer

Fill a cocktail shaker with ice

Add all the ingredients except the cream

Shake vigorously to combine and chill

Add the cream and shake briefly

Strain into a chilled coupe glass

Garnish with a light dusting of nutmeg

DONALD SUTHERLAND

CANADA

Donald Sutherland is a Canadian variation on the traditional Rusty Nail, which uses Scotch whisky. It's named for Donald's love of a rye whisky cocktail. I grew up watching him in *M*A*S*H* and *Kelly's Heroes*, a movie in which he plays the aptly named Sergeant Oddball alongside iconic stars such as Clint Eastwood and Telly Savalas. For this cocktail, I'd like to suggest an audio pairing in honour of Donald: the closing theme to *Kelly's Heroes*, 'Burning Bridges' by the Mike Curb Congregation. It's available via your streaming platform of choice and it's a winner to while away the hours while you're sipping the very spirit of Donald himself.

45ml (1½oz) Canadian rye whisky

22.5ml (¾oz) Drambuie

Ice: Cubed and large cubed

Garnish: Lemon twist

Equipment: Mixing glass, long bar spoon, strainer

Fill a mixing glass with ice

Add all the ingredients

Stir gently to combine and chill

Strain into an old fashioned glass with one very large ice cube

Garnish with a twist of lemon

FISH HOUSE PUNCH

George Washington loved a drink and legend has it that Fish House Punch was his absolute favourite. Also known as the Philadelphia Fish House Punch, this cocktail is said to have been created in 1732 in the State in Schuylkill, an angling club in Pennsylvania. By 1885, Fish House Punch was so famous that *The Cook*, a weekly New York magazine, wrote: 'There's a little place just out of town, Where, if you go to lunch, They'll make you forget your mother-in-law, With a drink called Fish-House Punch.' To be honest, that wouldn't work for me, my mother-in-law Camilla is one of my favourite people of all time.

30ml (1oz) cognac

30ml (1oz) three-year-old Cuban rum

22.5ml (¾oz) peach brandy/liqueur

30ml (1oz) breakfast tea, brewed and chilled (or still water, if you prefer)

15ml (½oz) freshly squeezed lemon juice

7.5ml (¼oz) simple syrup (see page 12)

Sparkling water to top (optional)

Ice: Cubed

Garnish: Lemon slice and grated nutmeg

Equipment: Cocktail shaker, strainer

Fill a cocktail shaker with ice

Add all the ingredients

Shake vigorously to combine and chill

Strain into a collins glass filled with ice

Top with a splash of sparkling water if you wish

Garnish with a slice of lemon and a light dusting of nutmeg

BRANDY OLD FASHIONED

(WISCONSIN-STYLE)

UNITED STATES OF AMERICA

Switching out whiskey for brandy, this variant on the Old Fashioned is something of a state cocktail in Wisconsin. The story goes that during the Chicago World Fair, the Milwaukee contingent found a bad batch of European brandy and used California Brandy instead, which hit seemingly all of their spots. Taking it back home, its popularity drove it through the gates of this recipe, where it has resided in serene delight ever since. As ever, it's a great fun variant, and the story, while quirky, is incidental to a wonderful riposte to the Old Fashioned that deserves to be worshipped far beyond Wisconsin.

60ml (2oz) California brandy

Lemon-lime soda or soda water to top

3 dashes Angostura bitters

1 orange wedge

2 maraschino cherries

1 sugar cube or tsp sugar

Ice: Cubed or large cubed

Garnish: Orange-cherry flag

Equipment: Muddler, long bar spoon

Add the orange, cherries, sugar and bitters to an old fashioned glass and muddle

Fill the glass with ice (or add just one extra-large ice cube)

Pour in the brandy and top with the soda of your choice

Stir once to combine

Garnish with an orange-cherry flag

EL PRESIDENTE

It seems this cocktail was created in the early 1900s, most likely during the time of Cuban president Mario García Menocal (1913–21), when Americans were roaring over to the island to flee Prohibition. Señor Menocal's fame has since dwindled, rather like another of Cuba's fascinating residents, the leaping crocodile. These reptiles can reach more than 3.5m in length, with scary agility and speed as well as pack-hunting instincts which set them apart from other crocs. Take a leaf out of the leaping crocodile's book and seek this cocktail in company – jumping and biting is entirely optional.

45ml (1½oz) three-year-old Cuban rum

22.5ml (¾oz) dry vermouth

7.5ml (¼oz) orange curaçao

7.5ml (¼oz) freshly squeezed lime juice (optional)

2 dashes of grenadine or grenadine syrup (see page 12)

Ice: Cubed

Garnish: Cocktail cherry

Equipment: Cocktail shaker, strainer

Fill a cocktail shaker with ice

Add all the ingredients

Shake vigorously to combine and chill

Strain into a chilled coupe glass

Garnish with a cocktail cherry

CANTARITOS

Hailing from Jalisco in Mexico, this Cantaritos recipe is a must for fans of the Paloma (see page 228). With its differentiating spritz, this zesty cocktail is often served in a Cantaritos clay pot in Mexico, which you can find online – alternatively, just use a collins glass.

60ml (2oz) reposado tequila

60ml (½oz) freshly squeezed orange juice

15ml (¾oz) freshly squeezed pink grapefruit juice

7.5ml (½oz) freshly squeezed lime juice

7.5ml (½oz) freshly squeezed lemon juice

Pink grapefruit soda to top

Pinch of sea salt

Ice: Crushed

Garnish: Lime wedge

Equipment: Mixing glass, long bar spoon

If using a Cantaritos clay pot, make sure you soak it in cold water for 15 minutes before using it

Three-quarters fill the pot or a collins glass with crushed ice

Fill a mixing glass with ice and add all the ingredients except the grapefruit soda

Stir gently to combine and chill

Strain into the pot or glass and top with grapefruit soda

Cap with crushed ice

Garnish with a wedge of lime

SANTO LIBRE

DOMINICAN REPUBLIC

Another variation on the Cuba Libre (see page 208), the Santo Libre is most likely named after the island's capital, Santo Domingo. White rum is the choice for this drink for its lighter flavour, and the Santo Libre is classically made with Brugal Blanco for its scented, coconut-like elegance. Experienced distiller Andrés Brugal Montaner founded the Brugal Company in 1888 and it has stringent quality controls to this day. Only using local molasses, the company insists on a minimum sugar content and purity of this key ingredient as well as using a special yeast strain that can ferment at higher temperatures than most. The attention to detail is laudable, and in this recipe I'm using Brugal Blanco Especial, which is a blend of Dominican rum aged in whisky barrels with the colour removed by charcoal filtering. It's a wonderful white rum with hidden mocha depth that gives the drink a bit more complexity, rather like a secret poem tucked between the folds of a greetings card.

60ml (2oz) Brugal Blanco Especial Dominican white rum

120ml (4oz) lemon-lime soda

½ fresh lime

Ice: Cubed

Garnish: Lime wedge

Equipment: Long bar spoon

Fill a collins glass with ice

Squeeze the lime half over the ice to extract all the juice and drop in

Pour the remaining ingredients into the glass

Stir once to combine

Garnish with a wedge of lime

THE CAESAR

(A.K.A. BLOODY CAESAR)

CANADA

Brace yourself for the full force of Canadian power. The Caesar is the de facto national cocktail of Canada – some 400 million are supposedly sipped by Canadians every year. It was invented in 1969 at the Calgary Inn, Calgary, where bartender Walter Chell took inspiration from the clams in the dish of spaghetti alle vongole – hence his addition of clamato juice. Sour, spicy, savoury and sweet all at once, this savoury brunch staple is a masterpiece.

45ml (1½oz) vodka

120ml (4oz) clamato juice

15ml (½oz) freshly squeezed lemon or lime juice (or a mix of both)

7.5ml (¼oz) Worcestershire sauce

7.5ml (¼oz) pickle brine

2 dashes hot sauce

¼ tsp celery salt

¼ tsp cracked pepper

Ice: Cubed

Garnish: Celery stick, dill pickles and red chilli

Equipment: Long bar spoon

Fill a collins glass with ice

Add all the ingredients

Stir gently to combine and chill

Garnish with a stick of celery, a speared pickle and a red chilli

CUBA PINTADA

CUBA

A popular variation on a Cuba Libre – its literal translation is 'stained Cuba', referring to the gentle hue of cola in this drink. The Cuba Libre is said to have been created in a Havana bar when a US soldier ordered Bacardi and Coke with lime and toasted 'Por Cuba Libre' to celebrate a free country. The rest, as they say, is history. But the Cuba Pintada is your future.

60ml (2oz) three-year-old Cuban rum

90ml (3oz) soda water

30ml (1oz) cola

Ice: Cubed

Garnish: Lime wedge

Equipment: Long bar spoon

Fill a collins glass with ice

Pour the ingredients into the glass

Stir once to combine

Garnish with a wedge of lime

MICHELADA

MEXICO

I first came across this Mexican marvel in Los Angeles and ever since it's been a welcome alternative to a Bloody Mary for brunch or hair of the dog. Beer instead of vodka brings the intensity down and the volume of tomato juice you add gives this liquid adventure a unique spin every time.

330ml (12oz) bottle chilled Mexican lager (light or dark)

120ml (4oz) tomato juice (optional)

15ml (½oz) freshly squeezed lime juice

3 dashes hot sauce

2 dashes Worcestershire sauce

Ice: Cubed

Garnish: Salt or Tajin rim and lime wedge

Rim a frozen beer mug with salt or Tajin

Add the lime juice, hot sauce and Worcestershire sauce and fill with ice

Top up with Mexican lager (or half tomato juice if you're using it)

Garnish with a wedge of lime

To make a Michelato, just switch out tomato juice for clamato.

ROFFIGNAC

This classic New Orleans cocktail seems to have been left by the wayside, which is a tragedy as it's as glorious as that moment in a disco when someone really good at dancing wiggles in a circle and everyone claps. Whether it's named after Cognac Roffignac, or the mayor of New Orleans between 1820 and 1828, Count Louis Philippe Joseph de Roffignac, this fruity red and gold drink is the taste of endless summers.

45ml (1½oz) cognac

75ml (2½oz) fermented raspberry shrub*

15ml (½oz) simple syrup (see page 12)

Soda water to top

Ice: Cubed

Garnish: Lime wedge

Equipment: Cocktail shaker, strainer

Fill a cocktail shaker with ice

Add all the ingredients except the soda water

Shake vigorously to combine and chill

Strain into a collins glass filled with ice

Fill with soda water

Garnish with a wedge of lime

* You can buy ready-made shrub but here's how to make your own:

Add equal amounts of champagne vinegar, raspberries and sugar to a clean and sterilized jar. Cover the jar and keep it somewhere cool and dark for about a month. Strain before using.

SAZERAC

This is one of a handful of cocktails to be trademarked – Sazerac rye whiskey must be used here, although since it's owned by the Buffalo Trace distillery, which I've had the pleasure of filming in, you might be forgiven for experimenting with Buffalo Trace bourbon. I'm sticking on the right side of the law though, since this is a New Orleans classic. If you get the chance to visit the city, this is a wonderful cocktail to sip in the local bars, and you could even visit the Sazerac House, which is dedicated to this fruity, mellow, silken drink as well as to the history of cocktail culture.

30ml (1oz) rye whiskey – Sazerac is the spirit of choice here

30ml (1oz) cognac

3 dashes Peychaud's or Creole bitters

2 dashes absinthe

Ice: Cubed

Garnish: Lemon twist

Equipment: Mixing glass, long bar spoon, strainer

Add 2 dashes of absinthe to a chilled rocks glass, then swirl around the glass and discard the liquid

Fill a mixing glass with ice

Add the remaining ingredients and stir gently to combine

Strain into the prepared rocks glass, adding more ice, if liked

Garnish with a twist of lemon

LAVA DOME

A stunning-looking cocktail, and tremendously tasty, it's the cousin of the Miami Vice – a bountiful blend of Strawberry Daiquiri and Piña Colada. Hawaii's Big Island is growing by more than 16 hectacres every year thanks to 30 years of the Kīlauea volcano's eruptions, and this cocktail will similarly expand into your life from the very first time you sip it.

30ml (1oz) three-year-old Cuban rum

30ml (1oz) coconut rum

60ml (2oz) cream of coconut

60ml (2oz) strawberry purée

60ml (2oz) freshly squeezed pineapple juice

½ ripe banana

Ice: Crushed

Garnish: Dehydrated pineapple slice

Equipment: Blender

Add the rums and strawberry purée (no ice) to a blender cup and pulse to mix

Pour this mix into a separate glass

Clean out the blender cup and add the remaining ingredients with 1 scoop of crushed ice

Blend on high to chill and combine

Pour both mixtures from opposite sides into a chilled hurricane glass

The strawberry mix will flow like lava through the cocktail

Garnish with a dehydrated slice of pineapple

PIÑA COLADA

Given that this was declared the official drink of Puerto Rico in 1978, the only question is, why have we not moved to Puerto Rico yet? It was created, so the story goes, by bartender Ramón 'Monchito' Marrero – so the next question we need to ask ourselves is, why doesn't everyone have a groovy middle moniker tucked between their names? My secret nickname was given to me by Levi Roots. He called me 'The Zebulon' and he still calls me Zebby to this day. Olly 'Zebulon' Smith it shall be. Please inscribe your name with groovy middle moniker in the space below:

60ml (2oz) three-year-old Cuban rum

75ml (2½oz) freshly squeezed pineapple juice

45ml (1½oz) cream of coconut

15ml (½oz) freshly squeezed lime juice

Ice: Crushed

Garnish: Pineapple wedge and cocktail cherry

Equipment: Blender

Add all the ingredients to a blender cup with 1 scoop of crushed ice

Blend on high to chill and combine

Pour into a chilled piña colada or hurricane glass

Garnish with a wedge of pineapple speared with a cherry

TORONTO COCKTAIL

CANADA

The best-selling whisky in America is not the local bourbon but Canadian whisky (spelled without an 'e') which by law must always be made from Canadian grain (e.g. wheat and corn) and aged for at least three years in charred oak barrels. Blends are popular, but rye whisky gets my vote for its spicy pep – which this cocktail is founded upon. The heritage of Canadian whisky stretches back to the migrants who had a good go at rum with imported molasses in the ports before becoming more reliant on growing grains as they journeyed from the coast. Whisky was often linked to flour mills, as they had the required access to grain; the first legal whisky distillery, Gooderham & Worts, popped up in 1832 in York – present-day Toronto. Today, Toronto is the largest city in Canada, encouragingly home to more than 10 million trees. This cocktail is dedicated to the one with the tastiest sap, the maple.

60ml (2oz) Canadian rye whisky

7.5ml (¼oz) Fernet-Branca

7.5ml (¼oz) maple syrup

2 dashes Angostura bitters

Ice: Cubed

Garnish: Orange twist

Equipment: Mixing glass, long bar spoon, strainer

Fill a mixing glass with ice

Add all the ingredients

Stir gently to combine and chill

Strain into a chilled coupe glass

Garnish with a twist of orange

GIN RICKEY

UNITED STATES OF AMERICA

Named after Washington DC Democratic lobbyist Joe Rickey during the late 1800s, the Gin Rickey is similar to a Tom Collins and great for those who prefer sharpness over sweetness.

60ml (2oz) gin

15ml (½oz) freshly squeezed lime juice

7.5ml (¼oz) simple syrup (see page 12)

Soda water to top

Ice: Cubed

Garnish: Lime wedge

Equipment: Cocktail shaker, strainer

Fill a cocktail shaker with ice

Add all the ingredients except the soda water

Shake vigorously to combine and chill

Strain into a collins glass filled with ice

Fill with soda water

Garnish with a wedge of lime

For a **Bourbon Rickey**, switch the gin for bourbon and omit the sugar syrup.

MAMAJUANA

DOMINICAN REPUBLIC

You can mix this with soda water and ice for a longer drink – it might be sensible considering its aphrodisiac reputation in the Dominican Republic. I make no claims in this department, but there are many additional spurious health benefits associated with the Mamajuana, such as cleansing the kidneys, liver, aiding digestion, enhancing circulation and banishing the flu. Could it also have the capacity to reverse the bodily landslide of natural ageing, I wonder? Surely these claims are all gibberish, so let's stick to the quality of flavour balanced in this concoction of rum, wine, honey and spices invented by Jesus Rodriguez of San Juan de la Maguana in the 1950s. However, even that story is cast into doubt by the suggestion that it's been around for 500 years among local shamans. So forget the tales – its divine, spicy smoothness is wonderful in winter, and if you can suddenly tell the future after drinking it, I'll happily settle for 15% of all future earnings.

600ml (20oz) red wine

600ml (20oz) Dominican dark rum

60ml (2oz) runny honey

3 star anise

2 tbsp chicory bark

2 agave leaves

2 cinnamon sticks

1 tbsp hibiscus petals, dried basil leaves and cloves

Fill a glass bottle or suitable storage container with the mix of herbs and spices

Pour in the wine, rum and honey and seal

Leave to steep for at least a week – the longer you leave it, the more the flavours are enhanced

Serve as a shot straight from the bottle

NEW YORK FLIP

UNITED STATES OF AMERICA

Flips are not usually made with cream – but this classic drink is, since New Yorkers are a creative, rule-bending bunch! There's something innately feelgood about flip cocktails, with their base of egg, sugar and booze. Around since the beginning of the Enlightenment in the late 1600s, flips are great for festive occasions – could be Thanksgiving, Christmas or just a special event in the cooler months, as their rich, glossy consistency is wondrous.

30ml (1oz) bourbon

22.5ml (¾oz) tawny port

15ml (½oz) single cream

15ml (½oz) simple syrup (see page 12)

1 egg yolk

Ice: Cubed

Garnish: Grated nutmeg

Equipment: Cocktail shaker, strainer

Add all the ingredients except the cream to a cocktail shaker without ice and shake hard to combine

Fill the shaker with ice and shake again to chill

Add the cream then shake briefly

Strain into a chilled cocktail or coupe glass

Garnish with a light dusting of nutmeg

QUEENS COCKTAIL

UNITED STATES OF AMERICA

This scrumptious, fruity cocktail is not to be confused with Queen Elizabeth II's favourite cocktail, which was a heady mix of one part gin and two parts Dubonnet. I met the late Queen when she named the P&O Cruises ship Britannia with my Glass House wine bar on board. I couldn't possibly reveal whether or not Her Majesty had a cocktail or two on that occasion. Let's just say the weather was dry, the celebration on board was suitably not.

45ml (1½oz) gin

22.5ml (¾oz) sweet vermouth

22.5ml (¾oz) dry vermouth

30ml (1oz) freshly squeezed pineapple juice

Ice: Cubed

Garnish: Pineapple wedge

Equipment: Cocktail shaker, strainer

Fill a cocktail shaker with ice

Add all the ingredients

Shake vigorously to combine and chill

Strain into a chilled coupe glass

Garnish with a wedge of pineapple

TIKI ESPRESSOTINI

UNITED STATES OF AMERICA

Technically, the Tiki Espressotini can be made with any coffee and liqueur combination. But Hawaii is famed for some of the finest beans in the business thanks to the Kona 'coffee belt' on the slopes of the Mauna Loa volcano. You'll pay a price for Kona coffee, but its sweet, bright acidity and intriguing complexity warrants comparison with a fine wine. And it brings this cocktail astonishing vibrancy. Thanks Hawaii, and here's also to your expanding world of mighty rums!

30ml (1oz) pineapple rum

30ml (1oz) Hawaiian coffee liqueur

30ml (1oz) freshly brewed espresso coffee, chilled

30ml (1oz) freshly squeezed pineapple juice

Ice: Cubed

Garnish: Coffee beans

Equipment: Cocktail shaker, strainer

Fill a cocktail shaker with ice

Add all the ingredients

Shake vigorously to combine and chill

Strain into a chilled cocktail glass

Garnish with 3 coffee beans

APPLETINI

UNITED STATES OF AMERICA

This 90s classic has made a real comeback in recent years, in part due to the film *The Social Network*. I have mixed feelings about social media. I lurk on Instagram @ollysmith and you can find me across all the digital realm in the same way as Appleton rum hides in plain sight behind every bar. The Appletini tends to be a bit of a room divider and there's even been hesitation from the bar community about fully embracing its popular appeal. As far as I'm concerned, if you enjoy an Appletini, drink it, make it, order it – and ignore the rest.

45ml (1½oz) vodka

15ml (½oz) sour apple liqueur

15ml (½oz) calvados

7.5ml (¼oz) freshly squeezed lemon juice

7.5ml (¼oz) simple syrup (see page 12)

Ice: Cubed

Garnish: Dehydrated slice of Granny Smith apple

Equipment: Cocktail shaker, strainer

Fill a cocktail shaker with ice

Add all the ingredients

Shake vigorously to combine and chill

Strain into a chilled cocktail or coupe glass

Garnish with a dehydrated slice of Granny Smith apple

FLAME OF LOVE

According to showbiz folklore, this drink was created for Dean Martin when he was drinking at Chasen's, a restaurant in Beverly Hills, and when Frank Sinatra tried it for the first time he loved it so much he ordered one for everybody in the restaurant. It certainly made its way into the world from Chasen's, whether or not with Dean and Frank's blessing, and it's a fabulous citrus Martini paying homage to Spain's fabulous fino. For a great widely available brand, use Tio Pepe – I was once asked by the team behind it to blend their top level Palmas sherries, affording me the honour of signing a barrel in the bodega. Not sure if they've honoured my request to be placed next to Sir Roger Moore's signed barrel. Either way I'd happily live forever inside a barrel as the liquid is so lovely.

60ml (2oz) vodka

7.5ml (¼oz) fino sherry

2 dashes orange bitters

Ice: Cubed

Garnish: Twist of orange and ground cinnamon

Equipment: Cocktail shaker, strainer, lighter

Add the fino sherry to a chilled cocktail glass. Rinse and discard the sherry

Fill a cocktail shaker with ice

Add the remaining ingredients and shake vigorously to chill

Strain into the prepared glass

Garnish by squeezing a twist of orange over a flame and then adding a dash of cinnamon

RUM PUNCH

BAHAMAS

One of my favourite things about the Caribbean is tracking down the differences in rum punch recipes. The cinnamon sprinkle at Sheer Rocks on Antigua was a revelation to me, but this Bahamian recipe is altogether simpler. It follows the lines of the easy-drinking 'real McCoy' rum punch you'll find blended in bars across the Caribbean. Captain 'Bill' McCoy is the chap behind this famous phrase – he was a notorious rum runner between the Caribbean and Florida during Prohibition, and his bootleg booze was particularly sought after as he didn't water it down. Hence, 'the real McCoy'.

60ml (2oz) Bahamian three-year-old amber rum

30ml (1oz) freshly squeezed lime juice

30ml (1oz) simple syrup (see page 12)

2 dashes Angostura bitters

Ice: Cubed

Garnish: Orange slice and ground cinnamon (optional)

Equipment: Cocktail shaker, strainer

Fill a cocktail shaker with ice

Add all the ingredients

Shake vigorously to combine and chill

Strain into a collins glass filled with ice

Garnish with a slice of orange (a dusting of cinnamon is optional)

CHI CHI

The Chi Chi – essentially a Piña Colada without the rum – was invented by Donn Beach, the legend behind a stack of famous cocktail recipes. Born Ernest Raymond Beaumont Gantt, this New Orleans lad owned the famous Don the Beachcomber's bar chain in Los Angeles and beyond. As well as inventing a heroic plethora of cocktails, Don was awarded military honours – a Bronze Star and a Purple Heart – during the Second World War.

45ml (1½oz) vodka

120ml (4oz) freshly squeezed pineapple juice

30ml (1oz) cream of coconut

Ice: Cubed and crushed

Garnish: Pineapple and cocktail cherry

Equipment: Cocktail shaker, strainer

Fill a cocktail shaker with ice

Add all the ingredients

Shake vigorously to combine and chill

Strain into a tiki glass filled with ice

Garnish with a pineapple wedge and a cocktail cherry

To vary this recipe and make a **Macadamia Nut Chi Chi** add 30ml (1oz) of macadamia nut liqueur for a richer, nuttier evocation of Donn's liquid heroism.

FROZEN MEZCAL PALOMA

MEXICO

Tajin is a mildly spicy seasoning for the rim of this cocktail – it is well worth bagging online if you're planning to make a bunch of these for a party. The Paloma is probably Mexico's favourite cocktail, and once tasted, it's easy to understand how it could edge the Margarita into second place. Using mezcal, Mexico's most traditional agave spirit, provides options given the vast range of flavours on offer from bottle to bottle. Unlike tequila, which can only be distilled from blue agave, mezcal can be made from around 50 different species of agave, which is roasted in pits or steamed. So you can often find smoky notes in mezcal – keep your eye out for the name Dangerous Don, he makes some outrageously tasty bottles.

45ml (1½oz) mezcal

60ml (2oz) freshly squeezed grapefruit juice

15ml (½oz) freshly squeezed lime juice

7.5ml (¼oz) agave syrup

Ice: Crushed

Garnish: Tajin rim and pink grapefruit slice

Equipment: Blender

Add all the ingredients to a blender cup with 1½ scoops of crushed ice

Blend on high to chill and combine

Rim a chilled old fashioned glass with Tajin (or salt if you prefer)

Pour the blender contents into the glass

Garnish with a slice of pink grapefruit

JAMAICAN COCONUT PUNCH

JAMAICA

In Jamaica, the coconut has been dubbed 'The Tree of Life' thanks to its extraordinary gift of finding its way into so many aspects of island culture – not least in a whole range of incredible cocktails, with this Jamaican Coconut Punch giving it a well-deserved starring role. Overproof 151 rum has a whopping 75.5% alcohol strength, and the varied deployment of coconut in this recipe is very much responsible for smoothing out any fiery edges. So take a calm breath and sip the Tree of Life's mellow bounty.

30ml (1oz) coconut rum

30ml (1oz) overproof 151 rum

120ml (4oz) coconut water

15ml (½oz) freshly squeezed pineapple juice

15ml (½oz) freshly squeezed lime juice

15ml (½oz) cream of coconut

Ice: Cubed

Garnish: Pineapple wedge and toasted coconut

Equipment: Cocktail shaker, strainer

Fill a cocktail shaker with ice

Add all the ingredients

Shake vigorously to combine and chill

Strain into a hurricane glass filled with ice

Garnish with a pineapple wedge and a light sprinkle of toasted coconut

RANCH WATER

This three-ingredient cowboy quencher was created in the dusty heat of West Texas. If you're a fan of an Aperol Spritz, give this tequila fizz a go. Topo Chico has quite a following, so much so that it was bought by Coca-Cola in 2017. It's been bottled in Monterrey, Mexico, since 1895, and rumours swirl about its magical properties, including curing an Aztec princess of something or other in the 1400s. One of these days perhaps I should create similar claims for my bathwater. Any mineral fizz will stand in just fine – I've suggested San Pellegrino, but for the full saline immersion, crack open a bottle of Badoit for outrageous salty impact.

45ml (1½oz) silver tequila

22.5ml (¾oz) freshly squeezed lime juice

7.5ml (¼oz) agave syrup (optional sweetener)

120ml (4oz) Topo Chico Mexican sparkling mineral water to top (San Pellegrino is a good stand-in)

Ice: Cubed

Garnish: Lime wedge

Equipment: Long bar spoon

Fill a collins glass with ice

Add the tequila, lime juice and agave if using

Fill with Mexican sparkling mineral water

Stir once to combine

Garnish with a wedge of lime

THE BROOKLYN

UNITED STATES OF AMERICA

Barbra Streisand, *Saturday Night Fever*, Jay-Z, Mel Brooks, *Moonstruck*, Al Capone, *On the Waterfront* and Jerry Seinfeld are all from Brooklyn. In spite of the name, this cocktail isn't. It was created by a Manhattan bartender named Jack Grohusko in the early 1900s – his only link to Brooklyn was that the restaurant's owner lived there! If you're a fan of the Perfect Manhattan (mixing sweet and dry vermouth), you'll be thrilled by your dalliance with the Brooklyn.

60ml (2oz) rye whiskey

15ml (½oz) sweet vermouth

15ml (½oz) dry vermouth

7.5ml (¼oz) Luxardo maraschino liqueur

7.5ml (¼oz) Amer Picon (or a dash of orange bitters)

Ice: Cubed

Garnish: Maraschino cherry

Equipment: Mixing glass, long bar spoon, strainer

Fill a mixing glass with ice

Add all the ingredients

Stir gently to combine and chill

Strain into a chilled coupe glass

Garnish with a speared maraschino cherry

HOTEL NACIONAL

CUBA

The Cuban hotel that lends its name to this creation is legendary. It has graced the centre of Havana since the 1930s with its art deco design; in 1946 it hosted a mob summit known as the Havana Conference, which is dramatized in Francis Ford Coppola's *The Godfather Part II*. As for the guest list over the years, it is quite heady – Fred Astaire, Buster Keaton, Rita Hayworth, Winston Churchill, Ava Gardner, Marlon Brando, Frank Sinatra, Nat King Cole, Walt Disney, Jean-Paul Sartre, Yuri Gagarin, Coppola himself, Steven Spielberg, Robert de Niro, Leonardo DiCaprio and Robert Redford. Johnny Depp is also a confirmed sighting, as my good friend Ellie and her mum met him in the Hotel Nacional's lobby in 1999.

45ml (1½oz) three-year-old Cuban rum

15ml (½oz) apricot liqueur

30ml (1oz) freshly squeezed pineapple juice

15ml (½oz) freshly squeezed lime juice

15ml (½oz) simple syrup (see page 12)

Ice: Cubed

Garnish: Dehydrated lime wheel

Equipment: Cocktail shaker, strainer

Fill a cocktail shaker with ice

Add all the ingredients

Shake vigorously to combine and chill

Strain into a chilled coupe glass

Garnish with a dehydrated lime wheel

P&P DAIQUIRI

This pineapple and papaya Daiquiri is a crescendo of tropical wonder that pays homage to these fine fruits that grow so scrumptiously in Hawaii. In an ideal world, only Hawaiian fruit would be used for this cocktail, especially since the pineapple locally symbolizes hospitality, welcome and happiness, for which the Hawaiian islands are rightly famed. If you don't mind using a pineapple rum from further afield, I'd be happy to recommend Plantation Stiggins' Fancy Pineapple rum, which is distilled then macerated with fresh pineapple from Trinidad & Tobago and seriously hard to beat. Islands unite! Hawaii, here's to you and all the joy you've brought to so many visitors from around the world. Aloha.

45ml (1½oz) pineapple rum

60ml (2oz) papaya purée (or flesh)

22.5ml (¾oz) freshly squeezed lime juice

15ml (½oz) freshly squeezed pineapple juice

7.5ml (¼oz) simple syrup (see page 12)

Ice: Crushed

Garnish: Papaya slice

Equipment: Blender

Add all the ingredients to a blender cup with 1 scoop of crushed ice

Blend on high to chill and combine

Pour into a chilled coupe glass

Garnish with a small slice of papaya

CHILIGUARO

COSTA RICA

Move over, Bloody Mary, it's time to summon the spirit of the mini-mighty Chiliguaro! Rangpur limes, originating in India and grown commercially in Costa Rica, are also known as mandarin limes or lemandarins. This piercing zinger is a hybrid of lemons and mandarins with the colour of a brand-new spacehopper from 1982. The taste is as memorable as Elvis Presley sky-diving into your cornflakes – however, if you can't catch Rangpur limes in your locale, pull the rip-cord on your quest and just use half lime juice and half orange juice, both freshly squeezed. The Chiliguaro offers a glimpse of why Costa Rica has been considered the happiest country in the world (according to the Happy Planet Index in 2019). 'Pura Vida!' as the locals say – pure life. I'll raise a glass to that, preferably with a refreshingly spicy and zesty Chiliguaro.

180ml (6oz) guaro (see page 262)

750ml (25oz) tomato juice

120ml (4oz) freshly squeezed Rangpur lime juice

60ml (2oz) hot sauce

Garnish: Salt rim

Add all the ingredients to a pitcher or sealable container (no ice)

Chill for at least 2 hours, longer if you can wait

Serve in chilled shot glasses rimmed with a little salt

QUEEN'S PARK SWIZZLE

TRINIDAD AND TOBAGO

Created in the 1920s in Trinidad's Queen's Park Hotel, with its grand bar and dashing setting, this glimmering star of a cocktail endures – as restaurant founder Trader Vic once put it, 'the most delightful form of anaesthesia given out today'. I know what Vic meant, but I actually find the Queen's Park Swizzle a pep to any day when drizzle threatens to burst into full rain song. Either way, its internal sunlight is about to rise in your heart.

60ml (2oz) three-year-old Cuban rum

22.5ml (¾oz) freshly squeezed lime juice

15ml (½oz) demerara syrup (see page 13)

2 dashes Angostura bitters

8 mint leaves

Ice: Crushed

Garnish: Mint sprig and lime wedge

Equipment: Muddler, long bar spoon

Muddle the mint in the bottom of a collins glass

Three-quarters fill with crushed ice

Add the remaining ingredients except the bitters and churn with a bar spoon

Cap with a little more crushed ice and dash the bitters over the top of the ice

Garnish with a sprig of mint and a wedge of lime

ESPANTO WAVE

BELIZE

Inspired by the Cayo Espanto Wave from the luxury barefoot island resort, this cocktail immediately makes me dream of the Great Blue Hole, a large underwater sinkhole off the coast of Belize that's well worth an internet search to behold. Forged in the last Ice Age, this circular chasm has all the qualities of a great cocktail – depth, intrigue and beautiful balance to its form. Make yourself an Espanto Wave and go mind-diving at once!

30ml (1oz) four-to-six-year-old Belize rum

22.5ml (¾oz) amaretto almond liqueur

15ml (½oz) blue curaçao

15ml (½oz) triple sec

60ml (2oz) freshly squeezed pineapple juice

15ml (½oz) freshly squeezed lime juice

7.5ml (¼oz) spiced rum (optional)

Ice: Crushed

Garnish: Pineapple wedge and cocktail cherry

Equipment: Blender

Put all the ingredients except the spiced rum (if using) in a blender cup with 1 scoop of crushed ice

Blend on high until you have a smooth, thick cocktail

Tap out into a collins glass and float the spiced rum on top

Garnish with a pineapple wedge speared with a cocktail cherry

ABSINTHE FRAPPÉ

UNITED STATES OF AMERICA

If you like liquorice, you'll love the Absinthe Frappé. It was invented at the Old Absinthe House bar in New Orleans in 1874 by Cayetano Ferrer; customers who adored this powerful potion included Oscar Wilde and Mark Twain. Traditional absinthe service with French dripping teaspoons or Czech flames can be a bit of a faff – this is an altogether simpler way of smashing right into it. For a drink with such notoriety, absinthe has worked its way into popular culture on numerous occasions; indeed, the 'Absinthe Frappé' is a show tune from the 1904 Broadway musical *It Happened in Nordland*, promising 'a dawning smile' as 'you imbibe your Absinthe Frappé'!

45ml (1½oz) absinthe

15ml (½oz) simple syrup (see page 12)

7.5ml (¼oz) anisette liqueur

Soda water to top (optional)

Ice: Cubed and crushed

Garnish: Mint sprig

Equipment: Cocktail shaker, strainer

Fill a cocktail shaker with ice

Add all the ingredients (except the soda water if using)

Shake vigorously to combine and chill

Strain into an old fashioned glass filled with crushed ice

Top with a splash of soda water if using

Garnish with a sprig of mint

CARAJILLO

MEXICO

Playa del Carmen on Mexico's east coast is the site of my fondest memory of this cocktail. The beach, the sunset, a great feast and the ultimate Carajillo, with its orangey-vanilla-coffee infusion among the 43 herbs and spices tucked into the duvet of deliciousness that calls itself Licor 43, originally from Spain. Exquisite to pep up your coffee, it's a contemplative gem of a drink. And if you're sipping late at night, consider decaf – unless you fancy pushing on till dawn, in which case I shall pull up a chair and happily join you.

60ml (2oz) Licor 43 Original

45ml (1½oz) freshly brewed espresso coffee, chilled

Ice: Cubed

Equipment: Long bar spoon

Add 4 ice cubes to a chilled rocks glass

Pour in the Licor 43 Original

With a bar spoon, layer the chilled espresso on top

Stir once before drinking

DAISY DE SANTIAGO

CUBA

Daiquiri fiends! Try this tart and floral riff on the big D. Chartreuse is the key addition – it's a totally underrated liqueur with a magical sunny tint that has been made by monks in France since 1840. The recipe is fused from more than 130 herbs and plants, with more sweetness and lower alcohol than green Chartreuse, lending gracious complexity to any cocktail. Since this particular example has been attributed to Facundo Bacardi and is served at the Bacardi distillery, you could use their white rum for this cocktail to honour the drink's origins, or stick to this recipe with a three-year-old rum to boost a gentle rumpus of richness.

60ml (2oz) three-year-old Cuban rum

7.5ml (¼oz) yellow Chartreuse

22.5ml (¾oz) freshly squeezed lime juice

15ml (½oz) demerara syrup (see page 13)

Ice: Cubed and crushed

Garnish: Mint sprig

Equipment: Cocktail shaker, strainer

Fill a cocktail shaker with ice

Add all the ingredients except the Chartreuse

Shake vigorously to combine and chill

Strain into a wine glass filled with crushed ice

Float the Chartreuse on top

Garnish with a sprig of fresh mint

REVERSE MANHATTAN

UNITED STATES OF AMERICA

This aperitif version of the Manhattan is an inversion of the classic recipe with sweet vermouth taking centre stage and whiskey on the back seat. Manhattans have been knocked back for nearly 150 years and will no doubt be around for centuries to come. Choosing the Reverse Manhattan before lunch is Rolex-accurate and catwalk-stylish.

60ml (2oz) sweet vermouth

30ml (1oz) rye whiskey

2 dashes Angostura bitters

Ice: Cubed

Garnish: Maraschino cherry

Equipment: Mixing glass, long bar spoon, strainer

Fill a mixing glass with ice

Add all the ingredients

Stir gently to combine and chill

Strain into a chilled coupe glass

Garnish with a speared maraschino cherry

OLLY'S TIKITOWN

TIKITOWN

This is the ultimate tiki drink – which is to say it's made with rum, a garnish of dreams, fruity exuberance and all-round fabulousness – from the made-up city of Tikitown. Inspired by listening to George Harrison's underrated album *Gone Troppo*, which has sunny tropical vibes billowing from every song, this cocktail is a homage to my all-time favourite track, 'Dream Away'. That track also plays at the end credits of *Time Bandits*, a favourite movie of mine growing up. So take yourself to Tikitown, stick 'Dream Away' on the stereo and do just that.

30ml (1oz) pineapple rum

30ml (1oz) three-year-old Cuban rum

15ml (½oz) apricot liqueur

15ml (½oz) Luxardo maraschino liqueur

45ml (½oz) freshly squeezed pineapple juice

22.5ml (¾oz) freshly squeezed pink grapefruit juice

15ml (½oz) freshly squeezed lime juice

7.5ml (¼oz) orgeat syrup

Ice: Cubed

Garnish: Pineapple leaves and maraschino cherry

Equipment: Cocktail shaker, strainer

Fill a cocktail shaker with ice

Add all the ingredients

Shake vigorously to combine and chill

Strain into a tiki glass filled with ice

Garnish with pineapple leaves and a maraschino cherry

MAGIC
MARGARITA

The inspiration for the Magic Margarita came during a session of tequila appreciation with my sister-in-law Cosi, which neither of us can remember terribly well. What survived into the dawn was a carefully drafted list of instructions for creating 'Magic Margaritas'. When put to the test, the recipe exceeded all expectations – put simply, it's ruddy scrumptious. The only mystery is who wrote it down, since the handwriting belongs to neither of us!

45ml (1½oz) reposado tequila

22.5ml (¾oz) St-Germain elderflower liqueur

60ml (2oz) freshly squeezed pink grapefruit juice

15ml (½oz) freshly squeezed lime juice

7.5ml (¼oz) agave syrup

Ice: Cubed

Garnish: Tajin or salt rim, lime wedge

Equipment: Cocktail shaker, strainer

Fill a cocktail shaker with ice

Add all the ingredients

Shake vigorously to combine and chill

Rim the collins glass with Tajin (or salt if you prefer) and fill with ice

Strain into the glass

Garnish with a wedge of lime

BARBADOS COCKTAIL

BARBADOS

I remember filming on a beach in Barbados enjoying a flying fish cutter – a local sandwich – while sipping on a cocktail that was packed with Velvet Falernum. This drink is liquid joy from the Caribbean – you could almost think of it like a whisper of rum infused with lime zest, cloves, ginger, cloves, almond, sugar and a few other secret spices. Rather than a lead singer, it's more of a backing vocalist giving a boost to the headline act, in this case five-year-old Barbados rum. It's hard to beat the beauty of Barbados, which is also known as 'Land of the Flying Fish' due to their plentiful numbers. If you get the chance, a flying fish cutter in hand alongside this cocktail is sheer bliss. Next best thing, make a fish finger sandwich and shut your eyes... you could almost be on Sandy Lane Beach.

45ml (1½oz) five-year-old Barbados rum

30ml (1oz) Velvet Falernum

22.5ml (¾oz) freshly squeezed lime juice

Ice: Cubed

Garnish: Lime twist

Equipment: Cocktail shaker, strainer

Fill a cocktail shaker with ice

Add all the ingredients

Shake vigorously to combine and chill

Strain into a chilled coupe glass

Garnish with a twist of lime

BIRD OF PARADISE GIN FIZZ

PANAMA

Similar to a Ramos Gin Fizz, this cocktail has an impressive head which rises up when the soda is added. This recipe takes a little practice – my tip is to shake it for longer than you think you should before adding the cream to the shaker. Sometimes credited to the Stranger's Club by the Panama Canal early in the 20th century, this classic reflects the extraordinary number of bird species across Panama's biodiverse landscape (more than 1,000, which is more than the USA and Canada combined) – with a special nod to the Bird of Paradise.

60ml (2oz) gin

30ml (1oz) freshly squeezed lime juice

22.5ml (¾oz) single cream

15ml (½oz) raspberry syrup

15ml (½oz) egg white

Soda water to top

Ice: Cubed

Garnish: Edible flowers

Equipment: Cocktail shaker, strainer

Add all the ingredients except the cream and soda water to a cocktail shaker (no ice) and dry shake to break down the egg white.

Fill the shaker with ice and shake vigorously to chill

Now add the cream and briefly shake to combine

Strain gently at an angle into a chilled highball glass, leaving room at the top to add the soda

Top with soda water

Garnish with an edible flower

MAMIE TAYLOR

A cocktail for fans of the Moscow Mule, with whisky making it richer and more smoky depending on the blend you use. I'll be grabbing Johnnie Walker Black Label, as it's so widely available and so darn good. The tale of this obscure cocktail, which was all but forgotten after Prohibition, unfolds along these lines: Mayme Taylor (the typo on the cocktail stuck) was an American operatic singer in the late 19th and early 20th centuries who ordered a claret lemonade after a day sailing on a lake. She was presented with something entirely different, which she rather liked and customized with a piece of citrus peel, which transformed it into her new favourite drink. The hotel manager immediately named this new cocktail in her honour, and this is my version. Cheers to Mayme; I hope this recipe makes you feel like singing when you make it.

60ml (2oz) blended Scotch whisky

22.5ml (¾oz) freshly squeezed lime juice

Ginger ale to top

Ice: Cubed

Garnish: Lime wedge

Equipment: Long bar spoon

Fill a highball glass with ice

Add the whisky and lime juice and stir

Top with ginger ale and stir once more to combine

Garnish with a wedge of lime

CANCHANCHARA

CUBA

You could think of the Canchanchara as a forerunner to one of my favourite cocktails, the Daiquiri (see page 234). Lime juice is absolutely central to electrifying the main line of both these cocktails and really gets those flavour wheels moving. In the case of the Daiquiri, I'm such a fan of the variations that I've created my very own Olly Daiquiri (see my *Home Cocktail Bible*, page 170). While the Mojito is said to be even older, the Canchanchara seems to have been catapulted to popularity by a bunch of freedom fighters active in the Cuban Ten Years' War (1868–78). With its origins laced with tales of battling for freedom, it's a strong drink to power you through your next setback. We shall overcome!

60ml (2oz) aguardiente

15ml (½oz) freshly squeezed lime juice

15ml (½oz) honey syrup (see page 14)

Soda water to top (optional)

Ice: Cubed

Garnish: Lime wedge

Equipment: Cocktail shaker, strainer

Fill a cocktail shaker with ice

Add all the ingredients except the soda water

Shake vigorously to combine and chill

Strain into an old fashioned glass filled with ice

Splash in a little soda water if you wish

Garnish with a wedge of lime

BROWN DERBY

Tart and sweet, and named after a diner in the shape of a hat, this cocktail is not brown – it glows an orange-gold and it is gorgeous! It apparently emerged in the 1930s in Hollywood's Golden Era from the Vendome Cafe at 6666 Sunset Boulevard, and the nearby Brown Derby diner, which was a haunt for local celebrities, is behind the name. You may never fancy eating your hat, but drinking it just became an unparalleled joy.

45ml (1½oz) bourbon

30ml (1oz) freshly squeezed pink grapefruit juice

15ml (½oz) honey syrup (see page 14)

Ice: Cubed

Garnish: Dehydrated pink grapefruit slice

Equipment: Cocktail shaker, strainer

Fill a cocktail shaker with ice

Add all the ingredients

Shake vigorously to combine and chill

Strain into a chilled cocktail or coupe glass

Garnish with a dehydrated slice of pink grapefruit

DE LA LOUISIANE

UNITED STATES OF AMERICA

De La Louisiane was the signature cocktail at La Louisiane restaurant in New Orleans and will appeal to fans of Sazeracs and Manhattans – it brings herbal flurries from the Bénédictine, a wriggle of sweetness from the vermouth and rumbling liquorice from the wingbeats of the green fairy, absinthe. A boozy blessing, this feels like drinking cocktails' greatest hits in one single serving.

45ml (1½oz) rye whiskey

30ml (1oz) Bénédictine

22.5ml (¾oz) sweet vermouth

7.5ml (¼oz) absinthe

2 dashes Peychaud's or Creole bitters

Ice: Cubed

Garnish: Maraschino cherries

Equipment: Mixing glass, long bar spoon, strainer

Fill a mixing glass with ice

Add all the ingredients

Stir gently to combine and chill

Strain into a chilled coupe glass

Garnish with 3 speared maraschino cherries

SPICED CUBAN SPRITZ

CUBA

Three of my favourite things are fizz, piquancy and rum. All of them together at once sounds like a nightmare with three heads. And yet the effervescence in this recipe is given depth by the spirit, and the chilli lurks at the centre of it all like a bullseye on a dartboard revealing a portal to the land of endless holidays.

45ml (1½oz) Cuban spiced rum

22.5ml (¾oz) freshly squeezed lime juice

15ml (½oz) demerara syrup (see page 13)

Champagne or English sparkling wine to top

Pinch dried chilli

8 mint leaves

Ice: Cubed

Garnish: Mint sprig

Equipment: Muddler, cocktail shaker, strainer, long bar spoon

Muddle the mint in the bottom of a cocktail shaker and fill with ice

Add all the ingredients except the champagne

Shake vigorously to combine and chill

Strain into a collins glass filled with ice

Top with champagne and stir once to combine

Garnish with a sprig of fresh mint

PINEAPPLE MOJITO

CUBA

This tropical twist on the classic Mojito was created in 2003 at Apartment 195, a bar on the King's Road in London, now sadly closed. You can vary the fruit as you please by changing the liqueur, purée and juice in the recipe. I love mango in my Mojito, and happily it's my wife Sophie's favourite fruit. With family in mind, I can hear my dear brother-in-law Zaman reminding me to celebrate the taste of Pakistani mangos – he's absolutely correct that they are stellar both in flavour and fragrance. And Cuban rum always deserves to be celebrated – whether it's the popular Havana Club or a lesser-known classy bottle such as Eminente ron de Cuba, it's the sacred fountain behind so many venerated cocktails.

45ml (1½oz) three-year-old Cuban rum

15ml (½oz) pineapple liqueur

45ml (1½oz) pineapple purée

1 lime, cut into quarters

8 mint leaves

Soda water to top

Ice: Crushed

Garnish: Mint sprig

Equipment: Muddler, long bar spoon

Muddle the mint and lime pieces in a collins glass

Three-quarters fill the glass with crushed ice and add the remaining ingredients except the soda water

Churn gently with a bar spoon to combine and chill

Top with soda water and churn once more

Cap with crushed ice

Garnish with a sprig of fresh mint

SECO NOLEM SOUR

PANAMA

You could pretty much describe Seco Herrerano as the national spirit of Panama. The sugar cane for this charcoal-filtered, clear rum is grown in the province of Herrera, which gives it its name. The title of this cocktail in turn comes from turning melon backwards from its mellow sweetness to a sharper cadence of zesty flair.

60ml (2oz) Seco Herrerano

30ml (1oz) watermelon syrup

22.5ml (¾oz) freshly squeezed lime juice

8 mint leaves

Ice: Cubed and crushed

Garnish: Lime twist

Equipment: Cocktail shaker, strainer

Fill a cocktail shaker with ice

Add all the ingredients

Shake vigorously to combine and chill

Strain into an old fashioned glass filled with crushed ice

Garnish with a twist of lime

JAMAICAN GUINNESS PUNCH

JAMAICA

The only thing more creamy and tropical than this cocktail is suntan cream. And since nobody needs a cocktail that coats you with factor 50 from the inside, this drink takes the prize. I love it with brunch – and before you start whispering 'hangover cure', it's simply a deluxe pick-me-up for any moment when you feel like something silky and spiffing.

360ml (12oz) Guinness

240ml (8oz) Dunn River Nurishment vanilla drink (or substitute with whole, almond, oat or any milk of your choice)

120ml (4oz) condensed milk

¼ tsp grated nutmeg

¼ tsp ground cinnamon

7.5ml (¼oz) vanilla extract

Ice: Crushed

Garnish: Whipped cream and grated nutmeg

Equipment: Blender

Add all the ingredients to a blender cup with 1 scoop of crushed ice

Blend on high to chill and combine

Pour into chilled collins glasses

Garnish with a swirl of whipped cream and a sprinkle of grated nutmeg

DOTTIE'S DELIGHT

BAHAMAS

This cocktail is a delectable taste of the 700 islands in the Bahamas, of which only around 30 are inhabited. This makes it a tempting location for movies such as *Pirates of the Caribbean* and *Silence of the Lambs*. It's also been a popular spot for James Bond to carouse around in *Thunderball, You Only Live Twice, Never Say Never Again* and *Casino Royale*. Nassau-born singer and dancer Dottie Lee Anderson inspires the name of this cocktail; the origins are shrouded in mystery but I like to think of Dottie sipping this drink with the sun glowing over the sea.

30ml (1oz) three-year-old Bahama amber rum

15ml (½oz) coconut rum

15ml (½oz) overproof 151 rum

15ml (½oz) Kahlúa coffee liqueur

90ml (3oz) freshly squeezed pineapple juice

15ml (½oz) freshly squeezed lime juice

Ice: Cubed

Garnish: Pineapple wedge and cocktail cherry

Equipment: Cocktail shaker, strainer

Fill a cocktail shaker with ice

Add all the ingredients

Shake vigorously to combine and chill

Strain into a collins glass filled with ice

Garnish with a pineapple wedge speared with a cocktail cherry

GUARO SOUR

COSTA RICA

Guaro is the drink of choice in Costa Rica and you'll find variations on the local Guaro Sour in every bar and restaurant. If you're partial to a Julep or Caipirinha, this taste of the tropics is for you. Ready to drink as soon as it's been distilled, guaro – short for 'aguardiente', meaning fiery water – is a clear spirit made from sugar cane. The most prominent brand is Cacique and if you find it hard to come by, you could deploy any neutral spirit in this recipe, from white rum to cachaça or even vodka – it'll still make you feel like a magic trumpet being played by the tropical breeze.

60ml (2oz) guaro

15ml (½oz) simple syrup (see page 12; or 1 tsp golden caster sugar)

1 lime, cut into 8 small pieces

Soda water to top

Ice: Crushed

Equipment: Muddler, long bar spoon

Muddle the lime and sugar syrup in the bottom of an old fashioned glass

Three-quarters fill with crushed ice and pour in the guaro

Churn gently with a bar spoon to combine and chill

Top with a splash of soda water and cap with a little more crushed ice

SWAMPWATER

UNITED STATES OF AMERICA

This cocktail was created in the 1970s by the US marketing team for Chartreuse. It was aimed at a more youthful market, so an alligator mascot was deployed along with the tagline: 'There's a little green fire in every sip of swampwater', which sounds to me like a one-way ticket to Indigestion Island. Still, I adore Chartreuse and happily, this cocktail is perfectly invigorating to sip. The combo of pineapple with Chartreuse is mesmeric.

45ml (1½oz) green Chartreuse

120ml (4oz) freshly squeezed pineapple juice

15ml (½oz) freshly squeezed lime juice

Garnish: Mint sprig and lime wedge

Equipment: Cocktail shaker, strainer

Fill a cocktail shaker with ice

Add all the ingredients

Shake vigorously to combine and chill

Strain into a collins glass (or mason jar) filled with ice

Garnish with a sprig of mint and a lime wedge

THE BRONX

Essentially a riff on the Perfect Manhattan. You can further play with the Bronx by substituting blood orange juice to make a Bloody Bronx, or for a Golden Bronx add an egg yolk to the shaker. A Silver Bronx is shaken with an egg white. The origin of the Bronx is lost to time, so let's just say the recipe was almost certainly not whispered on a nighttime breeze in New York around a century ago by the mysterious Lady Alice Bronx and her Melodious Moth Chorus.

45ml (1½oz) gin

15ml (½oz) sweet vermouth

15ml (½oz) dry vermouth

22.5ml (¾oz) freshly squeezed orange juice

2 dashes orange bitters

Ice: Cubed

Garnish: Orange twist

Equipment: Cocktail shaker, strainer

Fill a cocktail shaker with ice

Add all the ingredients

Shake vigorously to combine and chill

Strain into a chilled coupe glass

Garnish with a twist of orange

ANTIGUAN SMILE

ANTIGUA AND BARBUDA

My favourite memory of Antigua is strolling down Sir Vivian Richards Street. The only other star I've met with a street named after them is singer Tom Odell – it's in Chichester, since you ask, and technically Tom Odell Close is more of a car park than a street. Still cool though. Years ago I met Sir Vivian at Lord's in the Test Match Special commentary box. BBC host Jonathan Agnew had invited me to be a guest on the show, and if you've ever doubted the popularity of cricket, my phone didn't stop buzzing for days after the interview. Sir Vivian is one of the all-time great cricketers – his presence ripples with the calm power of a contemplative typhoon, and I warmly recommend watching the documentary *Fire in Babylon* to get a glimpse of this great man's reach, power and impact. But Antigua, which has a beach for every day of the year (hence the nickname Land of 365 Beaches) is also famous for its black pineapples, which are a rare sweet treat. They may look like any other pineapple, but the Antiguan black variety is imbued with a special kind of of deep deliciousness and the same could be said of the local fruity dark rum. In homage to these two brilliant ingredients, the Antiguan Smile is a true taste of the tropics. It's not obligatory, but I love to raise mine to the unofficial King of Cricket, Sir Vivian Richards.

45ml (1½oz) Antigua dark rum

30ml (1oz) crème de banane

120ml (4oz) freshly squeezed pineapple juice

15ml (½oz) freshly squeezed lime juice

Ice: Cubed and crushed

Garnish: Mango slices and black pineapple wedge (or use regular pineapple if the black variety is unavailable)

Equipment: Cocktail shaker, strainer

Fill a cocktail shaker with ice

Add all the ingredients

Shake vigorously to combine and chill

Strain into a hurricane glass filled with crushed ice

Garnish with slices of mango and a wedge of black pineapple

South America

BORGOÑA

CHILE

A great batch cocktail, often sipped during Chile's springtime fiestas. I first encountered it with a local camera crew when I was filming a documentary series about Chilean wine. They delighted in teaching me tongue twisters and colourful slang. As the drinks flowed I continued bungling the words into a surreal stream of joy-noise – I'll never forget the friendships born on that night! All thanks to the exuberance of this simple, fruity party drink.

750ml (25oz) Chilean red wine

60ml (2oz) Cointreau orange liqueur

12 ripe strawberries, halved

3 tbsp caster sugar

Ice: Cubed

Garnish: Edible flowers

Macerate the strawberries with the sugar in a pitcher or suitable container for 30 minutes

Add the red wine and Cointreau and chill for at least 4 hours

To serve, fill the pitcher with ice and serve in chilled glasses

Garnish with some edible flowers

CHICHA MORADA SOUR

PERU

Sweet and tangy chicha morada is a deep purple beverage made from the ckolli (a purple variety of corn), which grows in the Andes. Find it ready made online and revel in the drink's history, which stretches back to the days of the Incas and beyond. This is a decent cocktail for a wide range of food pairings thanks to its easy refreshment. I love it with a doughnut for a bit of indulgence, or for a savoury steer, skewered kebabs are the right kind of informal bite to pair this with.

60ml (2oz) pisco

60ml (2oz) chicha morada

22.5ml (¾oz) freshly squeezed lime juice

22.5ml (¾oz) simple syrup (see page 12)

Ice: Cubed

Equipment: Cocktail shaker, strainer

Fill a cocktail shaker with ice

Add all the ingredients

Shake vigorously to combine and chill

Strain into a chilled coupe glass

FERNET CON COCA

(A.K.A. FERNANDO OR FERNANDITO)

ARGENTINA

Fernet-Branca landed like a comet from the mind of Bernardino Branca into the cocktail glasses of Milan in 1845. With 27 mysterious ingredients, it was touted as a cure for pretty much any malady you care to mention – including cholera. One certainty is its enduring popularity in Argentina, where a distillery was established in 1925. Today, 75 per cent of world Fernet consumption is said to be in Argentina – their passion is impressive. I had my first Fernet Con Coca on the day I landed in Buenos Aires and found myself tangled in a beauteous barrage of on-street tango dancing. This cocktail is among the easiest to make and under the name 'Fernandito' is officially recognized by the International Bartenders Association. Feel free to play around with the ratios to your taste – some prefer a 50:50 mix, although this recipe is exactly how I remember it tasting all those years ago as the tango tornado whirled under a widescreen sky.

60ml (2oz) Fernet-Branca

180ml (6oz) cola to top

Ice: Cubed

Garnish: Lemon twist

Fill a collins glass with ice

Add the Fernet-Branca and top with cola

Garnish with a twist of lemon

BUENOS AIRES TELEGRAM

ARGENTINA

This is a family recipe with a romantic past. The cocktail wizard in my life is my friend Seb Munsch, whose ideas for drinks are as inventive and varied as Dolly Parton's wardrobe. Seb is married to Inez, and during the Second World War her grandmother, also called Inez, was living in Buenos Aires, where she met and fell in love with a British merchant seaman. Granddaughter Inez takes up the story: 'It was via telegram that he proposed to my grandmother. He insists that on that particular day there had been a special offer on the cost of the telegram. After he'd written his message he still had four words left to use, and being a man who wanted to get his money's worth, on a whim he decided to add "Will you marry me?". My grandmother's sense of adventure meant that she didn't hesitate to say yes. She hopped on a cargo ship to the UK and several weeks later landed in the UK where she began a long and happy life with my grandfather. After my grandfather passed away my grandmother got the chance to return to Argentina one last time. While she was there she drank cocktails and danced the tango in the streets of Buenos Aires. The Buenos Aires Telegram was created in their honour. My grandmother was partial to a whisky and ginger, and like any true sailor my grandfather always had a tin of Golden Virgina tobacco close to hand, hence the added smokiness.'

Let's raise our glasses in celebration of the beauty of romance. Cheers to love – and friendship.

45ml (1½oz) Monkey Shoulder blended malt Scotch whisky

22.5ml (¾oz) Stone's Original Ginger Wine

60ml (2oz) freshly squeezed orange juice

2 dashes rhubarb bitters

Ice: Cubed and large cubed

Garnish: Dehydrated orange slice and a smoked glass

Equipment: Cocktail shaker, lighter, woodchip, frying pan, strainer

---

Fill a cocktail shaker with ice

Add all the ingredients

Shake vigorously to combine and chill

Smoke the glass by lighting a woodchip in a pan and holding the glass over the top

Place a single large ice cube into the smoked glass and strain the cocktail over it

Garnish with a slice of dehydrated orange

EL CAPITÁN

PERU

My mate Jim Cook's nickname is El Capitán and he's the undisputed champion of fashioning cocktails while performing his 'crazy legs' dance moves. It's like watching a juggling octopus on rollerskates. The story goes that this cocktail got its name from the highlands that surround Puno when military captains would ride around demanding a pisco with vermouth – it's a tantalizing duet of bitter thrills. Very much like the morning after at Jim's house.

60ml (2oz) pisco

30ml (1oz) sweet vermouth

2 dashes Angostura bitters

Ice: Cubed

Garnish: Dehydrated orange slice

Equipment: Mixing glass, long bar spoon, strainer

Fill a mixing glass with ice

Add all the ingredients

Stir to combine and chill

Strain into a chilled coupe glass

Garnish with a dehydrated slice of orange

REFAJO

COLOMBIA

The soda Colombiana does not taste of cola, despite the fact it's also known as 'Kola Champagne'. It has more of a cream soda taste and works delightfully with barbecues, since it can handle all the smoke and marinades you throw at it. Dynamic froth with a compelling kick.

120ml (4oz) Colombian beer

60ml (2oz) Colombiana 'Kola Champagne' soda (or another cream soda)

30ml (1oz) aguardiente

Ice: Cubed

Fill a beer mug with ice and add the aguardiente

Top up with the beer and Colombiana soda (or cream soda)

CLERICÓ

URUGUAY

South America's answer to sangria, the Clericó is your new favourite cocktail for summer sipping. It is picnic perfection thanks to its effortless, light fruit finesse with a jazzy orange twist, and is hugely popular in Uruguay for parties and get-togethers. You can always make a batch and divide it into individual jam jars to serve with straws on the go; it's also a terrific cocktail for brunch.

750ml (25oz) white wine

90ml (3oz) triple sec or any orange liqueur

30ml (1oz) simple syrup (see page 12)

Soda water to top

250g (9oz) seasonal fruits (apples, orange, berries, kiwi etc)

Ice: Cubed

Garnish: Seasonal fruits

Equipment: Muddler, long bar spoon

Muddle the fruit in a pitcher with 30ml (1oz) of the triple sec and the simple syrup and leave for at least 30 minutes

Add the white wine and remaining triple sec and stir

Chill for 4 hours

To serve, fill the pitcher with ice and top with soda water

Pour into chilled glasses and garnish with extra fruit

CANELAZO

ECUADOR

Canelazo takes its name from the Spanish for cinnamon – canela. This hot drink is adored in the Andean highlands of Ecuador as well as cropping up elsewhere across South America. It's terrific for the toddy effect if you're feeling a little under the weather or need warming up outdoors – fireworks displays, winter walks or just at home for the portable fireside effect!

45ml (½oz) aguardiente

30ml (1oz) freshly squeezed orange juice

15ml (½oz) freshly squeezed lime juice

2 tsp caster sugar (or 15ml (½oz) simple syrup; see page 12)

1 cinnamon stick

240ml (8oz) water

Equipment: Saucepan

Bring the water, sugar, lime juice and cinnamon stick to the boil in a saucepan, then simmer for 2 minutes

Remove from the heat and add the remaining ingredients

Serve hot in a mug

CAPETA

BRAZIL

You've probably heard of a Caipirinha (see page 30), but have you ever tasted a Capeta? Capeta literally means 'devil', so this drink is also known as the Devil's Drink at Smith Towers. It's a real classic, especially in the north of Brazil, and is often shared at festivals and parties. Guarana powder is easy enough to come by at health food shops, and though I've never sprouted horns or found my hooves to be cloven after sipping a few of these, perhaps I just didn't look quite hard enough. Unleash your inner Capeta!

60ml (2oz) cachaça

60ml (2oz) condensed milk

15ml (½oz) honey

1 tsp ground cinnamon

1 tsp guarana powder (optional but recommended)

1 tsp cocoa powder

Ice: Crushed

Equipment: Blender

Add all the ingredients to a blender cup with half a scoop of crushed ice

Blend on high to chill and combine

Pour into a chilled highball glass

TERREMOTO

CHILE

Terremoto means earthquake, and as a volcanic region Chile gets its fair share. This cocktail may also make your legs tremble, so take it easy. Pipeño wine is young and rustic but you can make this with any good-value fruity white – try the peachy, mellow Viognier grape, or if you have a sweet tooth deploy a fruity rosé from California.

180ml (6oz) pipeño wine (or any ripe, fruity white or rosé wine will do)

30ml (1oz) Fernet-Branca

7.5ml (¼oz) grenadine or grenadine syrup (see page 12)

1 scoop pineapple ice cream

Add the wine to a chilled collins glass, then the Fernet-Branca and grenadine

Top with a scoop of pineapple ice cream or serve on the side. If you can't find pineapple, vanilla will do just fine

CHILEAN PISCO SOUR

CHILE

The battle lines drawn between Chilean Pisco Sour and Peruvian Pisco Sour are well established. I'm making no claim that Chile's is finer, but I did love drinking them when I lived there while filming a series for the local Canal 13 TV channel. My director Silvio Caiozzi became a good friend – I loved his wisdom, and he was an enigmatic cross between Vangelis and Kubrick. The first time I met him we drank Pisco Sours in the Ritz-Carlton Santiago. Within moments of meeting we connected, and with a raise of his glass he said: 'Olly, we will make this show together.' It was the fastest audition of my life and delivered an enduring friendship. Cheers to the Pisco Sour.

90ml (3oz) Chilean pisco

30ml (1oz) freshly squeezed limón de Pica (or lime) juice

1–2 tbsp icing (powdered) sugar (or 22.5ml (¾oz) simple syrup; see page 12)

Ice: Cubed

Equipment: Cocktail shaker, strainer

Fill a cocktail shaker with ice

Add all the ingredients

Shake vigorously to combine and chill

Strain into a chilled coupe glass

AGUARDIENTE SOUR

COLOMBIA

A must-taste for fans of the Pisco Sour. You could always substitute the aguardiente with white rum – ideally something sugar-cane based, but whatever you have to hand will still taste fabulous.

60ml (2oz) aguardiente

90ml (3oz) freshly squeezed orange juice

30ml (1oz) freshly squeezed lime juice

1 tsp caster sugar

15ml (½oz) egg white

Ice: Cubed

Garnish: Orange wheel

Equipment: Cocktail shaker, strainer

Add all the ingredients to a cocktail shaker and dry shake for 30 seconds to break down the egg white

Fill the cocktail shaker with ice and shake vigorously to chill

Strain into a chilled old fashioned glass

Garnish with an orange wheel

GANCIA BATIDO

ARGENTINA

Gancia is a light yet lush aperitivo, almost an easier-going sugar-coated white vermouth. It's wine-based, with a bittersweet balance and respectable booze level of 14.5%. If you've ever enjoyed a Pisco Sour – or indeed a sherbet lemon – and approve of apothecary levels of aromatics, this cocktail has got your name written all over it.

75ml (2½oz) Gancia (white)

30ml (1oz) freshly squeezed lemon juice

22.5ml (¾oz) simple syrup (see page 12)
    or 2 tsp caster sugar

Ice: Cubed

Garnish: Lemon slice

Equipment: Cocktail shaker, strainer

Fill a cocktail shaker with ice

Add all the ingredients

Shake vigorously to combine and chill

Strain into a highball glass filled with ice

Garnish with a slice of lemon

BOSSA NOVA

BRAZIL

There are various twists on the Bossa Nova cocktail – instead of pineapple juice, for instance, apple juice sharpens the drink with a pleasingly tart twist. I first encountered the music of bossa nova – which is derived from samba and has a melodious thread – via the 1967 album *Wave* by Antônio Carlos Jobim. The sound of the triangle alone is so mellifluous in the mix that your ears feel like they're gliding over the dreams of the very fairies themselves. Is it too far-fetched to say this cocktail is the liquid expression of such flowing splendour? You decide.

45ml (1½oz) three-year-old white rum

15ml (½oz) Galliano

15ml (½oz) apricot liqueur

90ml (3oz) freshly squeezed pineapple juice

15ml (½oz) freshly squeezed lime juice

Ice: Cubed

Garnish: Lime wedge

Equipment: Cocktail shaker, strainer

Fill a cocktail shaker with ice

Add all the ingredients

Shake vigorously to combine and chill

Strain into a collins glass filled with ice

Garnish with a wedge of lime

SUCUMBÉ

This is the perfect drink to feel fully snug when the weather gets frosty. If you love an eggnog, congratulations: you've just discovered your new favourite cocktail. Singani is a powerful yet scented Bolivian brandy distilled from Muscat of Alexandria grapes grown in soaring valleys stretching up beyond 1,600m (5,249 feet). It's Bolivia's national drink and since 1988, with the Bolivian Supreme Decree 21948, Singani has been declared an exclusive local product. It's well worth seeking out for the ultimate authenticity in this luxuriant libation.

60ml (2oz) Singani (or brandy, pisco or rhum agricole)

1 litre (35oz) milk

1 cinnamon stick

4 cloves

2 eggs

4 tbsp caster sugar

1 tsp vanilla essence

Garnish: Grated nutmeg and cinnamon sticks

Equipment: Saucepan, strainer, whisk

Add the milk, cinnamon stick, cloves, vanilla essence and half the sugar to a pan and warm gently (do not boil). Strain the milk to remove the spices and set aside to cool slightly

Separate the eggs and whip the egg whites to stiff peaks, add the remaining sugar and whisk again

Carefully add the egg yolks (one at a time) to the milk and whisk for a few minutes

Begin to slowly pour the milk mixture into your egg whites as you whisk

By now you should have a fluffy foam

Add 15ml (½oz) Singani to each glass and top with about a quarter of the foam

Garnish with a light sprinkle of nutmeg and a cinnamon stick

YUNGUEÑO

BOLIVIA

Taking its name from the humid Yungas Valley, this is a cocktail that's enjoyed by Bolivians from all walks of life. For this cocktail, I suggest your glass comes straight from the freezer, ensuring sub-zero refreshment for a blazing quench. It's equally at home in the sunshine or as a thrilling counterpoint to the world's hottest bath. I dare you.

60ml (2oz) Singani (or brandy, pisco or rhum agricole)

45ml (1½oz) freshly squeezed orange juice

22.5ml (¾oz) simple syrup (see page 12)

Ice: Cubed

Garnish: Orange wheel

Equipment: Cocktail shaker, strainer

Fill a cocktail shaker with ice

Add all the ingredients

Shake vigorously to combine and chill

Strain into a highball glass filled with ice

Garnish with an orange wheel

SERENA LIBRE

CHILE

A 90s cocktail invented in the bars of La Serena. I sat on the beach in this laidback northern Chilean city all evening waiting to see the green flash at sunset – the legendary moment the sun sparks a streak up the sky as it disappears. It was spectacular, despite the lack of greenery and flashing. A few days later I was interviewing an astronomer in the nearby observatory of Cerro Tololo in the Elqui Valley, who breezily remarked that the green flash was often visible from his back garden in La Serena. Later that day, this cocktail was a most welcome consolation, with the bright green surge of the limón de Pica lifting this drink through my mind to the top of the sky. To this day I still haven't seen the legendary green flash, though I do peer intently at all sunsets where there might be a lucky chance. In this drink, though, the inner green flash is perpetual.

60ml (2oz) caçhaca

60ml (2oz) papaya juice

15ml (½oz) freshly squeezed limón de Pica (or lime) juice

1 tbsp icing (powdered) sugar (or 7.5ml (¼oz) simple syrup; see page 12)

Ice: Cubed and crushed

Garnish: Papaya slices

Equipment: Cocktail shaker, strainer

Fill a cocktail shaker with ice

Add all the ingredients

Shake vigorously to combine and chill

Strain into an old fashioned glass filled with crushed ice

Garnish with slices of papaya

CHILCANO

PERU

Pisco is a bright, invigorating brandy distilled from grapes – if you love grappa, you'll adore pisco. The ginger, lime and bitters give this version of the world-famous Pisco Sour a real sense of lift-off – it's not rocket science, it's rocket fuel. Peruvians are rightly proud of their pisco, which comes from the coastal regions of Lima, Moquegua, Tacna, Ica and Arequipa. To be considered authentic it has to be neutrally aged for more than three months (generally in stainless steel or glass, so as not to impart flavour) and bottled in Peru. Real-deal pisco is bottled at distillation strength and additives are banned. It can only be made from Moscatel, Negra Criolla, Albilla, Torontel, Italia, Uvina, Quebranta and Mollar grapes, all of which deliver a certain nuance that can broadly be divided into aromatic and non-aromatic styles. If you see 'Puro' on the label, there's only one grape variety in it – for instance, Quebranta, Negra Criolla, Uvina and Mollar are decent bets for bright refreshment, whereas Moscatel, Albilla, Italia and Torontel are more aromatic and fruity. Mosto verde includes pisco that's been stopped before it's finished fermenting, which gives a certain sweetness – if you can find it, great fun for a velvet-smooth Pisco Sour. Acholado pisco is a blend of grapes and commonly used in a Pisco Sour – it's punchy stuff that's also fun for a cheeky shot to invigorate your eyeballs from within.

60ml (2oz) pisco

15ml (½oz) freshly squeezed lime juice

2 dashes Angostura bitters

Ginger ale to top

Ice: Cubed

Garnish: Lime wedge

Equipment: Long bar spoon

Fill a collins glass with ice

Add the pisco, lime juice and bitters. Stir once

Fill with ginger ale and stir once more

Garnish with a wedge of lime

BATIDA

Cachaça is Brazil's national spirit, and here this fine, clear, rum-like nectar is shaken into a creamy delight. This cocktail should be way more famous than it is.

45ml (1½oz) cachaça

60ml (2oz) coconut milk

15ml (½oz) freshly squeezed lime juice

7.5ml (¼oz) simple syrup (see page 12)

Ice: Crushed

Garnish: Lime wedge

Equipment: Blender

Add all the ingredients to a blender cup with half a scoop of crushed ice

Blend on high to chill and combine

Pour into a chilled highball glass

Garnish with a wedge of lime

You can add fruit to it if you feel like jazzing things up – just use 30ml (1oz) of any fruit purée or juice to create an instant disco.

TÉ CON TÉ

BOLIVIA

Literally, this translates as 'tea with tea', and served piping hot is a stalwart in my armoury of winter warmers. In Bolivia it's popular on the night of San Juan, one of the shortest and coldest nights of the year, often spent gathered around a barbecue. If you're in the UK, Bonfire Night or Winter Solstice are both fab dates to get this cocktail brewing, or indeed anywhere, any time you feel a little inner insulation is called for.

30ml (1oz) Singani (or brandy, pisco or rhum agricole)

½ tsp Bolivian black tea leaves

Cinnamon stick

Garnish: Lime slice and cinnamon stick

Equipment: Teapot

Boil a little water in a kettle or pan and measure off 120ml (4oz)

Add the tea leaves and a cinnamon stick to a tea pot and add the boiled water

Add the Singani to a mug, then strain the brewed tea into the mug

Garnish with a slice of lime speared with a cinnamon stick

GUARAPITA

VENEZUELA

I revere Venezuelan rum in the same way
that the sea is sacred to a lighthouse.
Diplomático is one of my personal favourites
to keep watch with thanks to its silky richness
and sumptuously sweet depth. For this cocktail
any decent rum will guide you to a safe port.
A Guarapita is great to serve in a pitcher –
multiply the servings according to the number
of people, as this version is simplified to serve
one. Have a play with the fruit juices too –
follow the beams of inspiration to wherever
you fancy. Mighty mango, glorious grapefruit,
entirely up to you to mix and match for the
most iconic combo.

45ml (1½oz) four-year-old Venezuelan rum

60ml (2oz) freshly squeezed orange juice

60ml (2oz) freshly squeezed passionfruit juice

15ml (½oz) freshly squeezed lime juice

7.5ml (¼oz) grenadine or grenadine syrup
(see page 12)

1 pineapple wedge

8 mint leaves

Ice: Crushed

Garnish: Dehydrated pineapple slice

Equipment: Muddler, long bar spoon

Muddle the mint and fresh pineapple in the
bottom of a collins glass

Three-quarters fill with crushed ice

Add the rum and grenadine then the fruit juice

Churn with a bar spoon and cap with
crushed ice

Garnish with a dehydrated slice of pineapple

Oceania & Australasia

SOLOMON ISLE COCKTAIL

SOLOMON ISLANDS

This gin-based cocktail is beloved in the Solomon Islands, which are almost 1,000-strong and home to East Rennell, the world's largest raised coral atoll, as well as Lake Tegano, the largest lake in the South Pacific. When you throw in the world's largest saltwater lagoon – Marovo in New Georgia – it's clear that the Solomon Islands are leading the liquid stakes across the region, not least with this scrumptious concoction. Sail the day away with it.

45ml (1½oz) gin

15ml (½oz) triple sec

15ml (½oz) cherry brandy

90ml (3oz) freshly squeezed pineapple juice

30ml (1oz) freshly squeezed passionfruit juice

15ml (½oz) freshly squeezed lime juice

Ice: Cubed

Garnish: Passionfruit half

Equipment: Cocktail shaker, strainer

Fill a cocktail shaker with ice

Add all the ingredients

Shake vigorously to combine and chill

Strain into a collins glass filled with ice

Garnish with half a passionfruit

JAPANESE SLIPPER

Despite the name this was invented in Melbourne by a French bartender named Jean-Paul Bourguignon back in 1984, the year the first Apple Macintosh personal computer hit the market, the Space Shuttle *Discovery* made its maiden flight and the year Frankie Goes To Hollywood roared around the UK charts for 70 weeks with 'Relax'.

If you love cocktails on the sweeter side this is totally for you. And if you love a good time, 'Hit me with those laser beams!'

30ml (1oz) Midori melon liqueur

30ml (1oz) Cointreau orange liqueur

30ml (1oz) freshly squeezed lemon juice

Ice: Cubed

Garnish: Maraschino cherry

Equipment: Cocktail shaker, strainer

Drop a maraschino cherry into the bottom of a chilled cocktail glass

Fill a cocktail shaker with ice

Add all the ingredients

Shake vigorously to combine and chill

Strain into the chilled cocktail glass

LEMON LIME BITTERS

(NON-ALCOHOLIC)

AUSTRALIA

Growing up on the island of Jersey, I used to drink this whenever I drove to the pub with my friends. At the time, *Neighbours* and *Home & Away* were all the rage, and in our late teens and early twenties, I think we secretly believed that in our surf gear and fading freckles we were trapped in some lolloping romantic soap saga that always turned out fine in the end. The Lemon Lime Bitters is a classy quencher thanks to its intriguing aromatic edge, and whether you believe it started as a cure for sea-sickness on board ships or just cascaded into Aussie culture thanks to its romping refreshment, it's a cracking glass to cool off with.

150ml (5oz) lemon-lime soda (or lemonade)

22.5ml (¾oz) freshly squeezed lime juice (or 15ml (½oz) lime cordial)

8 dashes Angostura bitters

Ice: Cubed

Garnish: Lime wedge

Dash the Angostura bitters straight into the collins glass and swirl. Do not discard

Fill with ice, add the lime juice and fill with lemon-lime soda

Garnish with a wedge of lime

For an alternative method, build the drink then dash the bitters on top to amp up the aromatic hit as you first sip the drink.

It's worth noting that Angostura bitters does contain alcohol, and while you're only adding a few drops, to be totally booze-free you could try exchanging it for a few drops of strongly brewed black tea.

Or, for slightly more of boozy hit, switch out the Angostura bitters for half a teaspoon of absinthe for a glass of subtle naughtiness.

KIWIMINTINI

NEW ZEALAND

New Zealand has a thriving kiwi fruit industry – the tart green zingers with their furry coats are electrifying in the intensity they bring to cocktails. What's more, they love being paired with fresh mint. It was one Mary Elizabeth Fraser who brought non-native 'Chinese gooseberry' seeds back to New Zealand in the early 1900s. The Cold War in the 1950s led to a search for a new name; 'melonettes' was rejected (The Melonettes – top name for a band), and while they're known all over the world as kiwis, this fruit from New Zealand is in fact largely marketed under the brand name Zespri. But as far as names go, it's hard to beat a Kiwimintini – wrap your tongue around it!

45ml (1½oz) gin

15ml (½oz) triple sec

15ml (½oz) freshly squeezed lemon juice

15ml (½oz) honey syrup (see page 14)

8 mint leaves

1 kiwi fruit, cut into quarters

Ice: Cubed

Garnish: Kiwi fruit slice

Equipment: Muddler, cocktail shaker, strainer

Muddle the mint and the kiwi fruit in the bottom of a cocktail shaker

Fill with ice and add the remaining ingredients

Shake vigorously to combine and chill

Strain into a chilled cocktail glass

Garnish with a slice of kiwi fruit

FRUIT TINGLE

AUSTRALIA

Evoking the classic Aussie sweets Fruit Tingles, this colourful cocktail is all about fun. If you've ever enjoyed the fruitiness of a Woo Woo, this is a similarly exuberant vibe – you just can't take it, or yourself, too seriously!

45ml (1½oz) vodka

30ml (1oz) blue curaçao

15ml (½oz) Chambord raspberry liqueur or grenadine or grenadine syrup (see page 12)

Lemon-lime soda to top

Ice: Cubed

Garnish: Lemon-cherry flag

Fill a hurricane glass with ice

Pour in the vodka, blue curaçao then the lemon-lime soda

Float the raspberry liqueur or grenadine (it will drop down through the cocktail)

Garnish with a lemon-cherry flag

FIJIAN FLIRT

Plantation Isle of Fiji Rum is a good bet for this cocktail, with its deep fruitiness and sweet spice a result of maturation both in bourbon casks and French oak casks. You can substitute with any good-quality golden rum to flow with the tropical exuberance of this finely balanced blend – it's great fun and terrifically tropical!

45ml (1½oz) Fijian rum

22.5ml (¾oz) orange curaçao

90ml (3oz) freshly squeezed passionfruit juice

30ml 1oz) freshly squeezed pineapple juice

30ml (1oz) guava juice

Ice: Cubed and crushed

Garnish: Passionfruit half

Equipment: Cocktail shaker, strainer

Fill a cocktail shaker with ice

Add all the ingredients and shake

Strain into a hurricane glass filled with crushed ice

Garnish with half a passionfruit

SOUTH SEA BREEZE

FIJI

South Sea Island is a small coconut-palm paradise in Fiji's Mamanuca Islands and it's been on my bucket list for decades. The gentle breeze from the aquamarine sea looks blissful as it ripples across the videos on my computer screen, enticing me to book a flight immediately! I will get to the island one day, but in the meantime, this is the cocktail to take you and I there directly via a single dream.

45ml (1½oz) coconut vodka

15ml (½oz) pineapple liqueur

60ml (2oz) guava juice

7.5ml (¼oz) freshly squeezed lemon juice

7.5ml (¼oz) honey syrup (see page 14)

Coconut water to top

Ice: Cubed

Garnish: Edible flowers

Equipment: Cocktail shaker, strainer

Fill a cocktail shaker with ice

Add all the ingredients except the coconut water

Shake vigorously to combine and chill

Strain into a collins glass filled with ice

Top with coconut water

Garnish with edible flowers

AUSSIE BEACHCOMBER

AUSTRALIA

Also known as Australia's answer to the Mai Tai, this is the cocktail to conjure the place where all Aussie legends converge... the beach. Whether it's a creek with a croc, blue threads of windswept surf, the distant scent of a barbie or a bustling shorefront bar, somehow there's a beach vibe to all Australian interactions. Maybe it's that laidback feeling of making everyone else feel at ease that seems etched into Australia's constitution of informality. Either way, this is the drink that I love to raise with the toast: 'Let's Be More Aussie.'

60ml (2oz) spiced rum

30ml (1oz) Cointreau orange liqueur

30ml (1oz) orgeat syrup

15ml (½oz) freshly squeezed lime juice

7.5ml (¼oz) honey syrup (see page 14)

6-8 mint leaves

Ice: Cubed

Garnish: Pineapple slice

Equipment: Cocktail shaker, fine strainer

Fill a cocktail shaker with ice

Add all the ingredients (no need to muddle the mint, the ice will bruise it as you shake)

Fine strain into a highball glass filled with ice

Garnish with a slice of pineapple

TAHITIAN VANILLA PUNCH

TAHITI

Tahitian vanilla is on another level. For its complexity and exotic intensity it can command high prices: *Vanilla tahitensis* is also a unique species. Each flower only blooms for a few hours, so the delicately precise task of hand pollination is a rare opportunity taken. Glossy, auburn and sizeable (sometimes 16cm/6in long) the vanilla pods are to be revered, with a typical plant producing only 50 to 100 beans per year. Let the magic beans cast their spell!

30ml (1oz) three-year-old Cuban rum

30ml (1oz) spiced rum

60ml (2oz) freshly squeezed orange juice

60ml (2oz) mango juice

7.5ml (¼oz) freshly squeezed lime juice

7.5ml (¼oz) Tahitian vanilla paste, extract or essence; if you can't find Tahitian vanilla paste use the best quality you can find

Ice: Cubed

Garnish: Dehydrated orange slice

Equipment: Cocktail shaker, strainer

Fill a cocktail shaker with ice

Add all the ingredients

Shake vigorously to combine and chill

Strain into a collins glass filled with ice

Garnish with a dehydrated slice of orange

HOKEY POKEY SHAKE

NEW ZEALAND

Hokey Pokey is a famously delicious flavour of honeycomb-toffee ice cream from New Zealand, but for this recipe, any sort of honeycomb ice cream will work just as well.

45ml (1½oz) honey bourbon

22.5ml (¾oz) milk

3 scoops Hokey Pokey (honeycomb) ice cream

Ice: Crushed

Garnish: Whipped cream and chocolate shavings

Equipment: Blender

Add all the ingredients to a blender cup with half a scoop of crushed ice

Blend on high to chill and combine

Pour into a chilled collins glass

Garnish with a swirl of whipped cream and a sprinkle of chocolate shavings

If you're in the UK you could always garnish with a Crunchie bar for some additional chocolatey crackle!

SYDNEY SUNRISE SUNSHINE

(NON-ALCOHOLIC)

AUSTRALIA

This very simple iconic Aussie breakfast drink is, according to legend, great for recovering from a hangover. An even better cure is, of course, to avoid the hangover altogether, but there's no doubt this Sydney classic is a vibrant romp to reset your body clock if it's feeling sluggish. And while pairing it with your favourite late-morning brunch is a great shout, this cocktail's vibes are enhanced even further by sipping it while listening to 'Southern Sun' by Boy & Bear – my all-time favourite Australian band and a gentle groove to restore rhythm to your day.

120ml (4oz) freshly squeezed orange juice or blood orange juice

30ml (1oz) freshly squeezed lime juice

22.5ml (¾oz) honey

1 egg

Ice: Crushed

Garnish: Orange wheel

Equipment: Blender

Add all the ingredients to a blender cup with 1 scoop of crushed ice

Blend on high to chill and combine

Pour into a chilled highball glass

Garnish with an orange wheel

LUSCIOUS LAMINGTON

AUSTRALIA

Cake, chocolate and coconut, the lamington is as Aussie as kangaroos, Kylie and cricket. Yes, I know cricket is international, but one of my all-time favourite sports memories was watching women's international one-day cricket at the Melbourne Cricket Ground on 19 January 2014. For some reason I'd been entrusted with a little Lego SpongeBob Squarepants mascot – I think by the England Women's Ashes team, who I'd been hanging out with, but there's a possibility my daughters back home put him in my care for the trip. Either way, England won by seven wickets and I celebrated with a lamington on the way back to my hotel. The whereabouts of Lego SpongeBob is unknown, but the lamington is locked firmly in Aussie culture – it's even got its own national day of celebration, marked Down Under every year on 21 July.

22.5ml (¾oz) vanilla vodka

22.5ml (¾oz) coconut rum

22.5ml (¾oz) Baileys Irish Cream

30ml (1oz) cream

Ice: Cubed

Garnish: Chocolate sauce and desiccated coconut

Equipment: Cocktail shaker, strainer

Gently dip the rim of a chilled coupe glass in chocolate sauce then into desiccated coconut

Fill a cocktail shaker with ice

Add the remaining ingredients

Shake vigorously to combine and chill

Strain into the rimmed coupe glass

INDEX